FIRESIDE

To Joe & Mom,
Love,
Patty, Susana
& Tony

and I thought I was crazy!

Judy Reiser

Illustrations by Randall Enos

A Fireside Book
Published by Simon and Schuster
New York

A Fireside Book

Published by Simon and Schuster
A Division of Gulf & Western Corporation
Simon & Schuster Building
Rockefeller Center
1230 Avenue of the Americas
New York, New York 10020

FIRESIDE and colophon are trademarks of Simon & Schuster

Designed by Stanley S. Drate

Manufactured in the United States of America

   3 4 5 6 7 8 9 10

Library of Congress Cataloging in Publication Data

Reiser, Judy.
  And I thought I was crazy!

  (A Fireside book)
  1. Curiosities and wonders. I. Title.
AG243.R345   031'.02   80-15360
ISBN 0-671-25399-9

Acknowledgments

Thank you, Moshe Lachter, for your invaluable belief, encouragement and advice.

I'm also grateful to Lillian Friedman, Linda Sunshine, John Linder, Richard Kahn and Irene Cohen.

And a special thank you to all my contributors.

to my mother and father
szeretettel és hálával

Warning:
The contents of this book
may be
highly contagious!

Foreword

So, all these years you were ashamed of yourself for kissing your socks goodnight. Nonsense. You shouldn't be ashamed at all. You shouldn't go around bragging about it either.

This book is not attempting to solve, define, or make excuses for some of the more common or uncommon idiosyncrasies. It is simply designed to help you recognize them, laugh at them, and breathe a little easier. It should serve in comforting you that you're not the only one who checks the change slot in public telephones for extra dimes or who touches the wall behind a "Wet Paint" sign to see if it really is.

It will allow you to accept or at least acknowledge that we are all loaded with meshugas (a Yiddish word for strange, unexplainable, inconsistent behavior). When you see that silver-haired, pin-stripe suited Wall Street banker type, it is quite possible that he, underneath all that normal exterior, is a total loono-wacko like you. Look, some of us wear our suits on the outside, others inside. That's life.

This sudden awareness will take a lot of your time. In fact, after reading this compilation of strange but absolutely true goings-on, you will be amazed that hardly an hour in your life goes by that you don't witness some of these quirks . . . either in yourself (who me?) or in others.

We know children have them. And in older folks, society chalks up odd and peculiar behavior to senility. If that's true, then senility begins at three years old. Of course having this marvelous copout, the old folks get away with this stuff like crazy . . . like crazy?

You'll finally understand your friends, enemies, bosses, husbands, wives, and lovers a lot better. You may even decide to adopt some of the more ingenious ideas here.

You'll have more tolerance for your tennis partner when he insists on using the same ball he just faulted with for his second serve and the game is held up for twenty minutes while you both look for it.

Quirk compatibility is essential among couples. The next time you're at a party, instead of asking, "Are you a Leo?", find out whether he's a Folder or a Crumpler. It's a good way to avoid serious problems in a relationship.

This book is really for entertainment. Have a good time. Laugh. Chortle. And gasp at the quirks people are involved in. It will make your behavior seem all right. Or, on the other hand, it will point out to you how sick you really are and depress the hell out of you. Should that happen, don't worry. Just wave your hands wildly over your head, wash an avocado with soap and water, and stick it in your ear. That always works for me.

and **I** thought
I was crazy **!**

Potpourri

It isn't Mental Cruelty that's the primary cause of broken marriages. Nor is it Adultery, Abandonment, or Habitual Drunkenness. The first and foremost cause is Toilet Paper. And the second is Toothpaste. If she likes it going over the front of the roll and he likes it going over the back or if she squeezes the tube from the middle and he squeezes from the bottom, those are grounds for divorce in my book. What did you think "Irreconcilable Differences" meant, anyway?

God help you if you're the wife of an almost Yul Brynner. I'll bet you a years supply of Vitalis that you can't get your foot through the door because he's in there carefully arranging his three strands of hair (which are each twelve inches long and parted at the neck) trying to cover the maximum territory. Just tell him that there's no such thing as a receding hairline, only a very high forehead.

And you can't flush your habits away. They're an important, distinctive, wet n' wild part of you, so accept them. Don't worry about what people would think if they saw you in the tub with your rubber duck (quirk, quirk). It's also acceptable to be a Reader or a Non-Reader, a Single-Flusher or a Double-Flusher, a Caruso under the shower or the Silent Type. Under no circumstances is it acceptable, however, to leave the toilet seat up in the middle of the night or the shower on when the water is turned off. Remember that.

What you do behind closed bathroom doors is my business. Both Howard Johnson and I know about those towels you stole on your last vacation. (C'mon, admit it.) Although I did try to be discreet and not touch on sensitive areas, I have to draw the shower curtain somewhere.

By the way, it doesn't matter how you squeeze the toothpaste, it all comes out in the end.

In my estimation, there are three different types of people: The Folders, The Crumplers, and The Rollers. The Folders are very immaculate. That's the way they are in real life. I'm a Folder, my wife's a Crumpler and my sister is a Roller. (That's when you hold onto it and roll it around your hand.)

Ticket Agent, airline, male, 32

Every day when I wake up and go to the bathroom to relieve my bladder, I go through the same ritual. As I'm peeing, I say out loud, "Only five days to go." There's always five days to go to something and I don't know quite what I'm referring to. It must have originated when I was in junior high school. I probably woke up one Monday morning and said, "Only five days to go," and felt very comfortable as I said it. It was reassuring to know there were only five days to go. Except I'd say it on Tuesday, Wednesday, Thursday and Friday, also. And now, I still say it in the morning. In fact, some of my friends have realized the beneficial aspects of this and some of them have tried it.

Mathematician, male, 29

I have an electric razor. Every morning after I shave, I look into the razor head to find out exactly how many whiskers are caught in the little blade, even though I don't clean it out.

Page, male, 22

I always use the same stall in the men's room at work. The second to the last on the right. It's the one I started with, so I just continue to use it. All of a sudden, bong, it occurred to me that I always use the same one.

Graphic designer, male, 29

A friend of mine keeps a cigar in the bathroom. Whenever he finishes using the toilet, he'll light the cigar, take a few puffs and leave. That's the only time he ever smokes.

Typographer, male, 36
His friend is a manager, plumbing supply
concern, male, 36

When I take a shower, I have a fear that a snake or some kind of reptile will come up through the pipes so I close down the drain. I usually have to take a medium to short shower as a result and end up with water up to my knees but I definitely manage to do away with the snakes.

Student, male, 22

After I go to the bathroom, I have to take a shower or I feel dirty all day long. I've never gone to the bathroom at work because I can't take a shower there.

Executive, garment center, male, 41

The problem with the toilet paper and the paper towels is that I like it hanging on the outside and the maid likes it hanging on the inside. So every week she comes and hangs it on the inside and when I get home, I take it off and hang it on the outside. We have this running battle.

President, advertising agency, male, 35

If the toilet paper is hanging off the inside of the roll, I must change it so that it's hanging off the outside otherwise I won't use it. This applies to all bathrooms, public or private, wherever I am.

Writer/producer, female, 33

No man likes to have anyone use his razor. My wife doesn't understand that. I tried buying her the same razor I use but it didn't help. She thinks my razor is better because I use it. I tried switching. I thought that if I took the razor I bought for her and put it where I usually keep my own, she would think it was my razor and use it. It didn't work. She always finds my razor no matter where I hide it. She often drops my razor and forgets to tell me so I cut myself or she leaves it in the shower and I can't find it. It's exasperating.

Family therapist, male, 52
His wife is a vice president, phone equipment
company, 46

If the water is not running, I can't go. Public bathrooms drive me crazy because I can't leave the faucet on. If I'm going straight home after work or somewhere where there is a normal bathroom, I'll save it.

Copywriter, female, 25

My friend dries his toothbrush every morning because he hates when the excess water dribbles off the brush and leaves a white film on the side of the toothbrush rack. He's meticulously clean. He recently got married and now he dries his wife's toothbrush too because she refuses to do it.

Graduate Student, male, 26
His friend is a graduate student, male, 26

My wife loves to watch television sitting on the pot. We have a television set in the bathroom and she watches all the soap operas in there.

Plumber, male, 43
His wife is a housewife, 34

I like to play my guitar sitting on the pot. I do my best playing there.

Musician, male, 23

I have a telephone in the bathroom. I don't tell the people I'm speaking to where I'm speaking to them from because many would be offended.

Gemologist, male, 27

I always flush the toilet twice because I think the bathroom will be cleaner and fresher.

Secretary, female, 44

When I was growing up, every person in my family used a towel a day, seven days a week. Of course, my mother did the laundry. It wasn't until I got to college, after I started living with other people, that I realized that some people use one towel for the entire week. I found that very strange because I was packed off to college with a huge trunk filled with towels. I was very quickly changed of that habit, however, when I started to do my own laundry.

Marketing director, publishing, male, 30

I squeeze the toothpaste directly into my mouth, not on the toothbrush. Then I zoom into the kitchen where I put the coffee machine on. Then I rush back into the bathroom and shave after which about fifteen minutes have elapsed and I still have the toothpaste in my mouth. At this point every morning I brush my teeth.

Wholesaler, womens' apparel, male, 35

I shave the same parts of my face in exactly the same order every day. I discovered this just the other day. I started to shave another way and I had disfunction, I just couldn't do it.

Attorney, male, 27

I wash my face and brush my teeth before going into the shower. I feel very dirty going into the bathtub or shower without having done that. In fact, once I took a shower without first brushing my teeth and washing my face and I felt so dirty that I got out of the tub, brushed my teeth, washed my face and then took another shower.

Professional fund raiser, female, 27

I won't drink any water at all from the bathroom sink, only the kitchen sink. To me, in my mind, it's different water. It could never be as clean because I associate it with toilets.

Housewife, 36

I get up two or three times during the night and go into the bathroom and brush and floss my teeth. I'm very particular about my teeth. I've always been that way. I take constant care of them, twenty-four hours around the clock.

Cosmetologist, male, 29

I assumed everyone in the world brushed their teeth with hot water. It never occurred to me to use cold water. I wash my face with warm water so it seems only natural to brush my teeth with warm water.

Marketing director, publishing, male, 30

It always seemed to me that seeing one little toothbrush in a holder for six looked very sad so I fill them all up with tooth-brushes. I have two bathrooms so I have ten or twelve tooth-brushes. All different colors. I always use the same one, the rest of them just sit there.

President, ad agency, male, 35

Every time I comb my hair, I comb my eyebrows. It's part of combing my hair.

Hairdresser, male, 23

After my girlfriend shaves her legs, she jumps into bed because she loves the way the sheets feel against her shaven legs.

Salesman, gift shop, male, 20
His girlfriend is a student, 23

I think it's vile to have a roll of toilet paper. I use Kleenex. It's much more civilized.

Hair colorist, male, 28

Even though I live by myself and there's no one else in the apartment, I close the door and usually lock it when I take a shower or go to the bathroom. I think it's because I saw "Psycho" and if someone should come into the house without my knowing it, hopefully, they won't see me or hurt me!

Teacher, remedial math, female, 29

I wash soap. I like to get all the bubbles and dirt off so it looks nice and clean in the soap dish.
ME: Do you dry it?
No, it dries by itself.

Publicist, male, 53

Ever since I've been old enough to stand up, I've pissed outside because it feels better, it's more natural, and it keeps the sewage system from clogging up. Urine is actually an excellent fertilizer when used in the proper ratio, and if I were ecologically conscious, I'd spread it around more but I concentrate on one area in front of my house because I'm shielded from the street there. Unfortunately, all the vegetation has burned to death. In the wintertime, I try to write my name in the snow. Frequently, I can only get the first two letters out.

Copy chief, newspaper, male, 37

I shower from the bottom up. I start with my feet and very systematically work my way up until I get to my head and wash my hair. Otherwise I would be stuck with the confusion of where I should start and it would throw my day into a turmoil. This system is not without its problems. The big disadvantage is that the dirt from my hair drips down and contaminates the rest of me which is already clean. But when I started this habit, I wasn't aware of the philosophical implications and now I can't break the habit.

Student, male, 20

For many years I brushed my teeth and shaved in the bathtub. I decided it took too long so I grew a beard and have been able to give up shaving. Now all I have to do is brush my teeth which I do in the shower. I have saved a great deal of time and added a couple of weeks to my life, I'm quite sure!

Lawyer, male, 32

Even if there's a cup around, I don't use it to rinse my mouth after I brush my teeth. I put my head directly under the faucet and take a big slurp and rinse only once.

Marketing analyst, female, 22

I always make sure, when I'm going somewhere, to bring a fresh roll of toilet paper with me. I use them as tissues, because they last forever. I get strange looks when people see me taking out a roll of toilet paper in public.

Student, male, 20

It's much more comfortable to be naked when going to the bathroom. I do this whenever I can, always in my own home. I'd like to be able to do it more often.

Businessman, 34

I've always wanted to tell somebody this. When I take a shower, I dry myself from the bottom up. I've always known it to be strange but it's a habit I do automatically without thinking. Now, at this age, it's the kind of thing I want to hold onto because it distinguishes me.

Housewife, 34

The only way I used to be able to go to the bathroom was to remove all my clothing, including underwear, jewelry and socks. It was the only way I used to feel absolutely comfortable, and still do really. I didn't start to work on curing it until I got to college. I had no choice. It would have been terribly embarrassing in the dorm if people had seen a pile of clothing lying on the floor. It's still a quirk at home. One of my brothers does it too. He's thirty-three and he's been doing it all his life.

Page, male, 21

When I go to the john, I take my ring and watch off. I put them on the counter and when I'm finished I put them back on.
ME: Why?
I haven't the foggiest.
ME: Have you lost many rings and watches?
Never.

Attorney, male, 35

I take off my pants and hang them up when I go to the bathroom at work. They're good pants and this way I can sit down, relax and read the paper without worrying about getting them wrinkled.

Executive, male, 39

I must have my second cup of coffee in the bathroom each morning before going to work. In fact, I bring the coffee, cigarettes, and ash tray and some reading material in with me and spend about fifteen minutes in there. I drink my coffee, smoke, and read as I go. Everyone calls the bathroom Jack's Library.

Mailman, 30

I know a woman who never uses a bath towel to dry off with. She uses a wash cloth and keeps wringing it out. It takes her about twenty minutes to get dry.

Writer, female, 29
Her acquaintance is an amanuensis for a
wealthy woman, female, 48

I flush the loo before and after. I really don't know why.

Striptease artist, female, 32

I only weigh myself stark naked, first thing in the morning before eating anything and after, hopefully, eliminating any wastes from my body and never with wet hair. Psychologically, my head feels better with the "the thinnest number."

Office manager, female, 31

Whenever I rip a piece of toilet tissue off, I fold the loose end of the roll a certain way so it looks tidy. What I do is fold both sides of the last square under and in toward the center to form a point, like the shape of an envelope flap. The toilet paper is hanging over the outside of the roll. Then I roll it back so it sits on the top of the roll and won't open. It gives it a neat finishing touch.

National manager, brewery, male, fifties.

I have hand towels to be used to dry only my face but any other part of me has to be dried with a separate bath towel.

Stylist, female, 28

Someone in my office uses four fresh towels every time she showers. One for her feet, one for her body, one for her face and one for her hair. Each time she uses a set of towels, she'll throw them in the wash. She won't reuse them.

Attorney, male, 34
His colleague is a secretary, female, 22

I have seven sets of towels, each in a different color. I pick a different color set every day according to my mood.

Textile designer, female, 23

I never use soap. I haven't bought any in years. I use the suds from the shampoo to wash my body after I've washed my hair. It gives me nice highlights—all over my body.

Partner, ad agency, male, 48

When I brush my teeth, I don't hang around the bathroom. I like to walk around the house and do different things like look at the newspaper or watch television. I don't like to stand in one spot. When I get enough lather in my mouth, I go back and rinse. I've never been able to figure it out.

Psychology student, female, 27

If there's anyone else in a public toilet, I won't go. I'll just wash my hands and leave so he doesn't think, "What is this weirdo coming into the bathroom for." I have very clean hands! In fact, I started college when I was fifteen years old and when I went out there, I wasn't worried about being away from home, I was worried about what the bathrooms were like in the dorm. I was afraid they wouldn't be private enough. When I got there it was even worse than I thought. All the bowls were lined up— they didn't even have stalls so for the first six months I went to the bathroom in the gas station across the street.

Controller, male, 31

I don't wash my hands after going to the bathroom in the upright position. If I'm somewhere where there are people I know and they can hear, I'll simply turn the water on and let it run for a minute so it sounds like I'm washing my hands. In a public john, I don't bother, I just walk right out because I'll never see those people again.

Cabana boy, male, 21

I never take a bath because I hate to wash the ring around the tub.

Administrative assistant, female, 40

My friend Beverly needs music or serenading when she goes to the bathroom. We traveled in Mexico together and I had to stand outside the door and sing to her every time she went. The whole point is that she's embarrassed about any possible sound.

Financial analyst, female, 33
Her friend is a teacher for emotionally disturbed
children, 32

I dry my face with the side of the towel that has the label on it and my body with the other side. Or, if the towel has two different textures, I'll use the smooth side for my face and the rough side for my body. That way, I don't have to use a separate face towel and I have a lighter load to wash.

Lawyer, female, 34

I hold my pocketbook on my head in a public bathroom and stand over the bowl and pee like a man. You would think I had a penis but, of course, I don't.

Housewife, 36

I don't like to be alone in a room with a closed door, so I leave the bathroom door open wherever I am.

Female, 80

Whenever I walk out of a bathroom, I always check to see if I have any toilet paper stuck to my shoe. I once had an embarrassing experience . . . I walked out of a bathroom with a long piece of toilet paper attached to my shoe and ever since I always make sure I don't.

Receptionist, female, 19

I never, ever dry off in the bathroom after I shower. I put the towel around me and walk into the bedroom. For a good five or ten minutes I just sit on the bed and stare into space. Then I dry off and come back in the bathroom to hang up the towel. I just want to sit down immediately after my shower even if it means leaving a trail of water on the floor every night.

Legal assistant, female, 23

I have my own bathroom in the basement which no one else uses. When I wake up in the morning, I go downstairs to that bathroom in my pajamas, sit down on the bowl, and sleep for another ten or fifteen minutes. Then I get up and take care of morning functions like brushing my teeth and shaving.

Supervisor, corporate photo department,
male, 65

I am compulsively neat. My apartment is immaculate at all times. Everything is always in order. Lined up. Perfect. But I have one quirk that is totally in opposition to my personality. I must squeeze the toothpaste tube from the center. I do NOT, as would be expected, squeeze the tube from the bottom neatly toward the top. I just take my hand and squish it in the middle.

Copywriter, ad agency, female, 30

When we were in the service, my friend would put a wash cloth on his face every time he went into the shower because he couldn't stand the water hitting his face.

Account executive, male, 33
His friend is an accountant, 33

Usually I shower in the morning but when I do take a shower or bath at night, I have to change the sheets on my bed. For some reason when I'm clean, the bed has to be too.

Legal secretary, female, 31

I've noticed that my wife spits in the toilet bowl after she uses it. I really don't know if it's just a habit or whether there's a practical reason for it.

Cab driver, male, 42
His wife is a medical secretary, 40

Going to the bathroom in a public place can be a real problem sometimes. First of all, it's got to be immaculately clean and I still put about six layers of paper on the seat. Also I have to be in there alone. If those two conditions don't exist. I do my best to hold it in. There's nothing worse than having someone walk in just when I'm about to put the sixth layer on.

Dancer, female, 32

I tear a half "U" in my newspaper before I use a public toilet. Opened up, it has a hole that fits the seat perfectly. Trouble is, it leaves a reversed impression on my ass.

Fashion designer, male, 22

When I shampoo my hair, I shampoo my moustache at the same time. It gives it a nice, clean luster and a good smell.

Sales representative, male, 28

When I pee in a public bathroom, I stand as far away from the bowl as possible. Sometimes the people next to me get splashed because I'm usually about three feet away. I can't understand men who lean right over the urinal in $300 suits.

Owner, auto repair business, male, 34

I use extra toothpaste on my central teeth and brush the most there because that's the part that shows.

Marketing consultant, female, 33

I go berserk if there's a hair in the sink or bathtub. It has to be absolutely spotless. I live with a gorilla who's covered with hair which makes it very difficult. I follow him around picking up after him.

Student, female, 33

Many times I walk out of a bathroom and think for a second, "Did I flush the toilet?" It's rare that I don't because I've been trained to do so but I have to go back and check.

Investment banker, male, 46

No matter how urgently I have to go, whether it's at home or in the Port-O-San on the construction site, I have to go through a preparatory ritual before I sit down. First, I tear off a piece of paper four squares long and fold along the perforations into one square and set it on the counter. Then, I tear off three additional pieces of paper, each three squares in length folded into one and put those behind the first one. I use them in that order and if there's no counter, I hold them on my lap. I can't believe I admitted this. My wife doesn't even know about it.

Architect, male, 48

I have to use exactly four squares. If I tear off five squares, I have to tear one square off before folding and if I tear off three squares, I throw that paper away and start over.

Marketing researcher, male, 39

I wear my glasses in the shower so I can see what I'm doing.

Design director, advertising, male, 40

If you rub one side of my face going down, it would be smooth, but if you did it on the other side, it would be rough unless you rubbed in the opposite direction. It's because I shave one side down and the other side up. I just got used to doing it that way.

Attorney, male, 33

When I take a shower, I turn the tub part on and I wash my hands
and feet first. Then I turn the shower on.

ME: Why?

Because that's the way I take a shower!

Account executive, male, 25

I work up a sweat shampooing my hair, so when I come out of
the shower, I have to wash under my armpits again in the sink.

Executive, music industry, male, 55

Before I actually start brushing with toothpaste, I have to prepare
my mouth for the experience so I rinse it first. Plain water is nicer
as the initial taste.

Sales Agent, airline, female, 32

I wash my feet several times a day. I don't know whether it's in
excess. I do it to eliminate any odor and for comfort because it's
refreshing. It cools me off without taking all my clothes off and
hopping into the shower.

Puppet maker, male, 29

My girlfriend brushes her teeth whenever she eats. If we're in the
car and she eats a piece of candy or fruit, she'll whip out her
toothbrush and start brushing her teeth as we're driving along.

Instructor, male, 34
His girlfriend is a film maker, 28

I keep an extra toothbrush in the bathroom so it doesn't look as
though I'm living alone. If someone decides to come live with
me, I have a brand new, clean toothbrush for them.

Manager, plastics company, male, 52

As an unusual surprise one time, I filled the tub with Perrier
water and my wife and I took a bath in it together. It took about
a hundred bottles. I'd do it more often if it weren't so expensive.
It felt like a Jacuzzi out of a bottle.

Vice president, shoe company, male, 35

The minute I step into the bathroom in the morning, I turn the water on and don't turn it off until well after I'm finished brushing my teeth, combing my hair, shaving, etc. The sound of the water in the morning has a tranquilizing effect.

Typographer, male, 36

We were trained not to waste water in the Navy because there's a shortage on board ship. So we showered in sections. We'd soap up one part of our body and only open the faucet to rinse and then shut the water off as we soaped up another part and so on until we were clean. By force of habit, I still do it that way. My sister and brother-in-law came to visit one time. They were waiting for me to finish my shower in the morning so they could use the bathroom and they told me afterwards that they couldn't imagine what I was doing in there because they heard the water going on and off. It seemed very strange until I explained the reason.

Fireman, 33

When I'm all done with everything else in the bathroom, right before I'm ready to wash my hands, I turn off the light. It's automatic and just in the bathroom. I don't know why. When I leave, the light is already off.

Security guard, female, 19

SCORE:

Why not jot down, step-by-step, the results of your toilet training. That way, you'll have a list for comparison.

If you identify with less than seven of these—You're a little behind.

From seven to eighteen—It's as clear as toilet water. You either have a weak bladder, excessively clean teeth or you're doing entirely too much reading. You must be very well informed.

Over eighteen—You probably squeeze the toothpaste from the top down.

Funny money

There are a wealth of idiosyncrasies in this section because money is the root of a lot of quirks. Rich or poor, we've all got them.

If you have money to burn and you do it, you belong here. You've got what's known as an Extravagant Quirk. If your money is wrapped in foil and plastic and labeled Hamburger and you keep it in the freezer, you've got a Cold Cash Quirk. If you only buy it in a Downtown Discount Store at the end of the season on sale, you've got a Practical Quirk. If you only buy it in an Uptown Boutique at the beginning of the season at full price, you've got a Foolish Quirk. If you get someone else to buy it for you, you've got a Smart Quirk. If you thought this book was overpriced when you bought it, or worse yet, if you borrowed it and didn't buy it, shame on you, you've got a Don't-Know-A-Bargain-When-You-See-One Quirk.

Then there are those of you who file the contents of your billfold with a system more intricate and sophisticated than all the information at Merrill, Lynch, Pierce, Fenner & Smith. Oh, you didn't think that was a quirk? Think again. And you with the jars and cans and pots of pennies, you have a friend at Chase Manhattan. He's the only teller who'll put up with the 3,000 rolls you bring in once every two years. Actually, he looks forward to them. He saves them too. Some folks are always trying to get rid of their pennies. When the cashier rings up $3.98, they say quirkly, "Wait, I have three pennies!" It's called the Three Penny Opera. Let's not forget the guys who carry a wad of bills with Washington's picture on the outside. You can't fool me. I know *there are a lot of Jacksons and Hamiltons hidden in there. Ladies, don't laugh, some of you have quite a load in your brassiere and that doesn't mean your physical attributes.*

Anyway, read on and I hope you get your money's worth.

I'm crazy with bills. They must be in exact order, small bills first, large bills at the end, the heads facing in the same direction. The dirty bills are in front of the clean bills so I get rid of those first. More precisely, at the front of my wallet are the dirty one dollar bills, then the clean one dollar bills, then the dirty fives, then the clean fives, and so on.

Personnel director, female, 35

There are dozens of jars of pennies all over my apartment. I take the pennies out of my wallet at the end of the day and save them in jars. Although I think about cashing them in for dollars, I never do and just keep accumulating more and more jars.

Administrative assistant, female, 23

Every morning I take a dollar bill and separate it from all my other bills. I put it in the change compartment of my wallet instead of the bill compartment. In case of an emergency, I always have some hidden extra money.

Budget analyst, female, 30

Every night I divide my nickels, dimes, quarters and pennies in four cans. At the end of the month I usually have from two hundred to two hundred and fifty dollars worth of change. I go out and either buy myself something or do something stupid with it.

Marketing manager, male, 38

My aunt flicks each bill about five times to make sure she's only handing over one—even if it's to my uncle.

Student, male, 17
His aunt is a bookkeeper, 45

When my kids lose a tooth and I want to give them money from the Tooth Fairy, if I don't have a clean dollar bill, I iron an old one to make it crisp. I just have this thing about dirty money and I have to iron it if it's not clean and crisp.

Graphic designer, male, 38

My boyfriend keeps track of every penny, and I mean every penny, he spends. During the course of the day, he'll make entries in a special journal he carries with him for this purpose: restaurant—$41, transportation—50 cents. He can go back ten years and tell you how much money he spent on liquor in 1970. Everyone thinks he's cheap because he's constantly adding.

HER BOYFRIEND: It's a great way of budgeting and managing cash-flow. Plus I know what my net position is at any point in time. I can also tell you how much money I owe.

Security analyst, female, 26
Her boyfriend is an investment banker, 28

I always make it a point to know exactly how much money, to the penny, I have on me. It comes from a lifetime of scrounging for money.

Production manager, printing company,
male, 44

When I get paid, it must be in crisp, fresh bills. If it's dirty, I run from teller to teller until I get all new bills. Sometimes I even go to three banks in one day to get new bills. If I'm handed dirty money in change somewhere, I give it to my wife. Show her my clean money, Joan.

Executive, textile business, male, 37

When I first met my friend I thought she was a very open person because she would tell me absolutely everything about her sex life in gory detail. But it took me years to find out how much money she made for a living. That she refused to divulge.
ME: Is her salary as good as her sex life?
No.

Social worker, female, 36
Her friend is a secretary, 29

I round off the figures in my checkbook to the next highest whole number. If, for example, I write a check for $23.60, in my checkbook I would enter $24.00 dollars as the amount. If I realize I've forgotten to enter a check, I'll make up a figure which I think is higher than what I actually spent and subtract that. At the end of the year I can look forward to a lot of extra money left in my account.

Art director, female, 27

When I have to remember something, a device that I developed is that I hold a coin in my hand. If I have to remember one thing, I hold one coin. If I have to remember two things, I hold two coins.

Typographer, male, 36

I left my borsello [small leather bag] which contains my wallet and papers in a taxi. An attorney found it and was nice enough to call me. When I arrived at his office, he said, "I couldn't help but notice that your money was all loose and mixed up in your bag. The bills were in all directions, no denominations together. It was really bothering me so I straightened it out. That's the only thing I did to your bag. I hope you don't mind."

Retired, male, 41

The tail side of a coin has always been luckier for me. It's what I call when someone flips a coin. When I put change on a table or dresser, I turn all the coins tail side up.

Systems analyst, male, 33

I never cut the price tags off my rugs or wall hangings. Someone told me it was probably because I don't want the feeling of permanence and if I don't cut them off, it means I can move any time.

Accountant, male, 35

I always look down at the sidewalk when I'm walking to avoid stepping in dog shit and to find money.

Physician, female, 29

Sometimes I'll take a hundred dollar bill and put it in the refrigerator next to the bottle of ketchup. When I open the refrigerator at seven o'clock in the morning, the first thing I see is the hundred dollar bill. I have a feeling that it's possible to train yourself to increase your prosperity consciousness by getting used to seeing large sums of money in very common, ordinary places. I've taken a wad of money and thrown it up in the air, letting it fall all over the floor. I've put it on shelves and just let it sit there. After awhile, I get used to seeing it and I expect to see money everywhere.

Numerologist, male, 36

I throw pennies away because there's nothing I can do with them. They're useless.

Stockboy, male, 20
(I stopped him after I saw him throw them into the street.)

I'll buy something just to break a bill that's dirty so I can have fresh money. The thought of so many people touching money turns me off.

Diamond dealer, male, 55

Every time I cash my paycheck, I smell each bill before putting it in my wallet.

ME: Do they smell good?

Only the new ones.

Librarian, male, 23

I carry four pennies with me at all times so I have the exact change.

Designer, china and crystal, female, 24

I staple groups of money together and label them so I can keep track of them. More specifically, if I have forty dollars in my wallet and I withdraw another hundred dollars from the bank, that hundred dollars would be stapled together, labeled and set aside until the forty dollars are gone.

Film director, motion pictures, male, 31

I always make out a check for whole dollars and pay the cents in cash. If a bill is $35.10, then I'll make out the check for thirty-five dollars and hand over the ten cents. It makes my checkbook so much easier to balance.

Designer, china and crystal, female, 24

I'm a superstitious gambler. If I go to the track or play cards or gamble in any form, I must first discard all my pennies even if it means throwing them in the street. It's bad luck to have pennies when I gamble.

Construction superintendent, male, 50

When the first customer of the morning hands me my fare, I spit on the first coin or bill for good luck. I acquired this habit from a former boss of mine who was superstitious too.

Cab driver, male, 58

As far as money is concerned, I'll go to extraordinary lengths not to accumulate pennies in my change. If I go to a store and something costs $1.06, I'll give the cashier $1.11 so I'll get back one coin, a nickel, instead of giving her $1.10 and getting back four pennies in change. I just don't like to have that many objects to worry about.

Marketing manager, corporation, male, 27

Instead of just tossing my change on the dresser at night, I stack it neatly in a conical shape, with the largest coin on the bottom, and the smallest on top. If anyone knocks over my change, I get very upset and I have to stack it up again.

Traffic coordinator, ad agency, male, 22

God and I have a deal going. When He does something good for me, I do something good for Him. For example, I wanted to sell my car, so I told Him I'd put twenty dollars in the collection plate if I sold it. When I found a buyer, I followed through on my promise. I'm happy, He's happy—it's a wonderful system.

Court officer, male, 26

In our cash register, all the money is placed with the heads facing up and with the tops of the heads aimed toward the door. It keeps things in order.

Operator, candy store, male, 33

I buy things in even amounts. I'll buy $10.00 worth of gas as opposed to 5 gallons which may come to $8.92. When I buy clothes, I'll buy a $150 suit rather than one for $99 even if I like the unevenly priced one better. In a bakery, if an item is $1.00 per pound, I'll buy it no matter what it is instead of something that may be $1.79 per pound.

Vice president, television network, male, 30

It's very difficult for me to buy something that is not on sale. If two items are the same price, I'll buy the one that's been reduced rather than the one that's straight price. I'd almost go so far as to say that if I liked the straight priced one a little more, I'd buy the reduced one anyway.

Sales rep, advertising space, female, 35

I can't stand to be in the house with loose change in my pockets. The minute I get home, I have to empty my pockets.

Dentist, male, 52

Instead of ten nickels, I try to beat the system by putting only seven or eight in the bus coin machine. Luckily, I haven't been caught yet.

Collector, credit card company, male, 27

I have about twenty different bank accounts. I deposit checks from various sources in separate accounts. It's my way of keeping the books. I always know exactly how much money I've received from each particular source. And I would never use money from one source to pay another. I don't mix money.

Executive, retailing, female, 46

I keep my bills arranged so the presidential heads are facing each other and the tails are facing each other. I'm less apt to accidentally pull two out at the same time and mistakenly pass them for one.

Computer consultant, male, 36

Although the mail is only delivered once a day, as many times as I walk in and out of the house, I check the mailbox. I'm convinced that any day now they're going to bring me a special letter informing me that I won the big house or the big car or the $50,000 Reader's Digest Sweepstakes check.

Health administrator, male, 31

If I drop a nickel, dime or quarter, I'll bend down to pick it up. If I drop a penny, I don't bother, I just leave it and walk away.

Hairdresser, male, 31

Before my friend leaves work, he puts a subway token in his ear, where, apparently, it is securely held on his way to the station. He says that it keeps his hands free and he doesn't have to fumble at the turnstile.

Junior account executive, female, 21
Her friend is a short-order cook, male, 45

I keep the smaller denomination bills wrapped around the outside of the larger ones so it looks as if I have less money than I do. If I'm peeling money off, I'm peeling dollar bills off and it looks less ostentatious.

Attorney, pension insurance and tax,
male, "almost 35"

I get rid of old money first. I hate the way it feels. New bills are so nice and clean.

Serigrapher, female, 24

I divide my money into four separate envelopes in my pocket-book. It makes me feel like I have a lot of money.

Nurse, female, 39

Any change that I have left at the end of the day goes into a little cup. Periodically, I buy myself flowers with it and that's the only thing I'll permit myself to use it for.

Nurse, female, 34

SCORE:

There's more to money than spending it, saving it, earning it and worrying about it. This chapter will give you a new perspective on your pocket and everyone else's.

From zero to five similar—You're bearish on bread quirks. Feel free to experiment with some of these.

From five to ten—Count your blessings, you're average.

Over ten—Your bread is sourdough, you're a millionaire in quirks. Skip this chapter, you can't afford any more. Perhaps you should invest in some intensive psychotherapy.

Out to lunch

In this chapter you'll find everything from soup to nuts, mostly nuts.

Remember that girl you went out with who kept blowing her nose through the entire dinner. Wasn't that the best filet mignon you never ate? But then again, didn't she look at you a little strangely when you put some of the Ajax you brought with you into your glass of water and washed all your silverware? That was after you used your napkin to wipe your chair. Clearly, you are both suffering from classic, aberrational, gastronomical behavior. Or, in short, a culinary quirk. Other symptoms are:

1. Ordering peach melba as an appetizer.
2. Eating creamed spinach with your hands.
3. Keeping your laundry in the refrigerator.
4. Having spaghetti and meatballs for breakfast.
5. Your favorite thing to eat are shoelaces.

There is no known cure for these but don't go bananas. Your shrink is probably out to lunch too so forget about going there for help. If you find any of the above apply to you, here's what you can do in each situation.

1. Order matzo ball soup for dessert.
2. Sign up for a lifetime course with Amy Vanderbilt.
3. Don't invite me for dinner.
4. Wake up at 5 P.M.
5. Take out the White Pages, look under 'B' for Bellevue, dial the number and explain your problem.

It also helps to associate with people who can really appreciate your individual style. If you like to eat off of someone else's plate, find someone who enjoys eating off of yours. You love the egg white but hate the yellow? No problem. There are plenty of yokels around. Your quirk is that you're looking for a writer/art director with a good appetite to prepare a daily perfect gourmet dinner for after she comes home from a hard day's work? Very interesting. I can really appreciate your individual style.

Anyway, bon appétit.

Malomars. First I eat off the chocolate top, then the marshmallow and then the cracker part. Never, never would I bite into the whole thing at once. It would be obscene!

Furrier, male, 50

I bite off the ends of hot dogs and throw them out before I eat them. I just don't like the look of them. I do the same with pickles.

Assistant television producer, male, 36

I can tell whether or not dinner will be good when I come home and kiss my wife because she usually has some of it on her chin. If I don't like what I taste when I kiss her, I announce that I want to take her out for dinner. I get credit for being romantic and I get a good meal after all!

Proofreader, male, 36
His wife is a waitress, 29

If I'm eating alone, I must either read or watch television. I can't just eat. I've got to have something to occupy my mind.

Packaging broker, male, 45

I proportion each item on my plate so that if I don't complete something, there is an equal amount of everything left. My father eats the same way.

Stewardess, 25

I never let anybody, including my wife, wash my beer glass with soap, only salt water. The beer tastes better!

Elevator constructor, male, 52

This is an old meshugas of mine. I prefer stale bread to fresh bread because I eat less of it. There's always a big selection of old bread in the house and I always eat the oldest one. In fact, sometimes we throw away the newer bread!

Manager, tire factory, male, 58

I pick up the groceries in the supermarket in the order that they're written on my list. If the bread and the cereal are next to each other in the same aisle but not one after the other on my list, I will go past the cereal and come back for it later when I reach it on my list. Grocery shopping is like therapy for me. It's relaxing, I enjoy it and I take my time with it.

Actress, 28

I iron my lunch every once in awhile. If I want to have a quick meal without doing a lot of cooking, I put mushrooms, tomatoes, lettuce and cheese in a pita bread, tuck the ends in, wrap it in aluminum foil and iron both sides for four or five minutes. The cheese melts, the bread is nice and warm and I have a delicious sandwich.

Photographer, male, 43

When most people are served a hamburger, they will simply pick it up and eat it. I've noticed that when my wife and daughter pick up their hamburgers, they flip it over and eat it upside-down. It's absolutely phenomenal!

President, design firm, male, 37
His wife is a housewife, 35
His daughter is 14

I eat all around the outside of a sandwich first and then I eat the middle.

Wrangler, Colorado ranch, female, 21

It's very hard for me to go to a restaurant and not taste everyone else's dish at my table. And I usually sample theirs before I try my own.

Actress, 41

My girlfriend will insist on using the same teabag for her husband's cup as well as her own although I would be willing, naturally, to give each of them their own teabag.

Dental hygienist, female, 32

During a meal, I have to mix each of the elements on the fork each time I take a bite. For example, if dinner consists of meat, potatoes and a vegetable, a little bit of the meat, the potato and the vegetable will always be on the fork at the same time as I eat.

Student, male, 20

I like to eat food with my hands as much as possible. I especially like squishing mashed potatoes and ice cream. A couple of months ago, I broke a hand and it was fantastic having a legitimate excuse to eat that way in public and not be civilized in the least.

Gardener, female, 25

When I order dessert, I divide it in half and immediately put pepper all over one of the halves so I won't be able to eat it. This way I can have my cake and eat it, too, with half the calories.

Counselor for very ill patients and their families,
female, 31

My grandfather struck me as being peculiar when I went to visit my grandparents one summer in Kansas City. We were having breakfast and my grandmother pulled a pot off the stove and served him chicken gravy on his pancakes. I couldn't believe it. But he grew up on a farm in Kansas about the turn of the century and apparently they had no maple syrup there.

Researcher, library, male, 26

I don't like to eat on Friday nights because I like to be thin going into the weekend.

Houseplant broker, male, 34

My husband cannot sit down to any meal without adjusting the lighting. They're on dimmers and it usually takes him between five and ten minutes to play around with them. He'll sit down, start to eat, he'll decide that it's too bright, get up, dim them, sit down for awhile, then he may feel that it's too dark so he'll get up again to change the intensity.

Teacher, sex education, female, 35
Her husband is an industrial designer, 36

When I'm slicing up something like bananas or carrots, I have to eat the last piece. I've tried not to but it still ends up in my mouth!

Chartist, female, "thirty-plus"

When my boyfriend cooks, we cannot sit down to eat until all the pots have been washed. As a result, we very often have a cold hot meal.

Veterinarian, female, 36
Her boyfriend is a builder, 41

I drink coffee with the spoon in the cup. It's a Polish habit that I learned from my father.

Scheduling administrator, television, female, 24

I only eat black jelly beans because I love the licorice flavor. The other colors taste too sweet. They sell just the black ones but it's much more fun picking them out of the colored ones. I leave the rest of them for my secretary who likes jelly beans of any color.

Underwriting vice president, insurance company, male, 40

I never mix unmixed fruit-flavored yogurt. I just scoop down the side and dip each spoonful into the preserves on the bottom. Everybody asks me why I do it that way. They think it's strange but it's so much better. It tastes just like a sundae.

Student, female, 17

I don't like to hear people eat. If you and I were in a room together and you started to eat an apple, I'd tell you to stop or I would leave. In a restaurant there's so much noise, it doesn't matter. But if there's silence and the silence is broken by the sound of someone eating, I find it disturbing.

Salesman, 45

I can't eat with my eyeglasses on. The food looks too clear with them, I have to eat blurry.

Housewife, 33

I have a habit of eating cold cereal for breakfast and sometimes before I go to bed. Unless I'm eating the cereal with the exact same spoon, I just can't seem to be very happy eating it. I always search for that particular spoon.

Sales manager, electronics manufacturing
company, male, 45

I feel guilty eating a whole piece of cake so what I do is play a game with myself by going back and forth into the refrigerator and cutting very small slivers. I usually finish the whole thing and end up feeling guilty anyway.

Social worker, female, 33

Our daughter never finishes a meal completely no matter how hungry she is. She'll leave one bite of each item on her plate.

Conferee, male, 47
His daughter is a dental hygienist, 22

If there's one last bit of food left on a dish or tray, the last olive, or carrot, or piece of bread, I won't have it because it's bad luck. I also won't purchase the last item left on a supermarket shelf for the same reason.

Textile wholesaler, male, 33

When I was little, we had an argument about whether we should eat the vegetables or meat or the things we liked or disliked first. So I began eating my food in alphabetical order. You have to know how to spell, though.

Banker, male, 26

I eat all the green vegetables on my plate before any other item because I can't stand the color green.

Tennis pro, male, 23

My wife, Miriam, thinks that everything always tastes better off of my plate than off of hers. That way, it looks like she's eating like a bird!

Attorney, male, 32
Miriam is a speech pathologist, 30

When I get two sunnyside up eggs, I break one yolk and spread it over the white and eat that egg. Then I eat all the white around the second yolk being very careful not to break it. When all that's left is the second yolk, I plop it in my mouth whole.

Engineer, male, 66

If you'd come into the kitchen while I'm cooking, you'd see forks, spoons, utensils, plates and pots all over. If I'm mixing the peas, I'll use one spoon, if I'm making a sauce, I'll use another spoon or fork. If you'd come into the kitchen while George was cooking, you'd see one solitary utensil, a fork or spoon which he uses for everything. He eats with the same fork he cooks with. He uses the same plate for all his food. It's going into the same stomach, he might as well put it on the same plate. George is the kind of guy who doesn't like to waste things. You'd never see him throw away a piece of paper that doesn't have every space completely filled. On the other hand, I hardly write anything on a piece of paper before I throw it out. What's interesting is that we live together very well and we have such opposite habits.

Psychotherapist, female, 38
George is a manufacturer, handbags, 48

People who chew gum are not in existence as far as I'm concerned. If they talk to me, I look the other way and won't respond unless they remove the gum.

Fashion designer, female, 54

I mix all the food on my plate together. Everything I eat is a casserole or becomes one when it's put in front of me. It all joins together in the end anyway.

Art director, male, 30

I set a formal breakfast table for myself at night before I go to sleep. I put a tablecloth on the table and place a complete setting for one out. I get the pot and any utensils ready that I will need to cook with. I like to see my table set when I get up in the morning.

Executive secretary, female, fifties

I can't possibly eat a stuffed green olive without taking out the pimento and eating that first. The idea of just squishing into the whole thing is really boring.

Secretary, female, 25

I eat everything that does not require a knife with chopsticks. If I know someone well enough to bear my idiosyncrasy, I'll ask for chopsticks in their home as well. I frequently take my own with me to restaurants when I'm feeling secure. In a Chinese restaurant, if for some reason they don't have chopsticks, I won't eat there.

College professor, male, 38

Sometimes I eat before I go out to dinner with a date so I won't be famished and make a pig of myself.

Vocational rehabilitation counselor, female, 29

When I eat an ear of sweet corn, I butter, salt and eat three rows at a time. It always seemed logical—you don't get your fingers as sloppy. Consequently, it's very nice if the corn works out to have twelve or fifteen rows.

Airline pilot, male, 43

The lettuce has to be on top of the meat in a sandwich. If it's on the bottom, it just doesn't taste right. If I'm eating a sandwich in someone else's home or a restaurant and the lettuce is on the bottom, I turn the sandwich upside down.

Engineer, male, 22

Whether I'm having an elaborate meal or just an Oreo cookie, I like to eat by candlelight.

National manager, brewery, male, fifties

My husband doesn't like different foods to touch on his plate so he eats off an old steel army plate that has sections.

Housewife, 32
Her husband is a national sales manager,
corporation, 30

People find it strange that I line my refrigerator shelves with shelf paper. But I like things to be super clean and this keeps my refrigerator cleaner, longer.

Dental technician, female, 56

Sometimes I'll just have one bite and leave the rest but I absolutely must sample the cheesecake in every restaurant that I go to. In fact, I had to give up Chinese restaurants because they don't have cheesecake.

Copywriter, female, 25

When my father wants a piece of fruit, like an apple, he'll cut it in half, eat half, put the other half in the fridge, go back and get another apple, cut that in half and only eat half of that one. The other halves eventually go bad and get thrown out.

Graduate student, female, 24
Her father is a businessman, 64

I love the taste of salt and there isn't anything that I eat that I don't salt first. I would salt a salty bagel. There's no such thing as too salty!

Embroidery designer, female, forties

I once had a girlfriend who would only eat seven string beans. She would give me a whole heap of string beans, but on her plate there were only seven. I used to call her Seven-string Bean Mary.

Art director, male, 39
His ex-girlfriend is a graphic designer, 29

I rotate my dishes, silverware, and glasses so they all wear evenly. More specifically, I have a service for eight and if three of them are washed and five are left in the cabinet, I can't take the three that are clean and put them on top of the pile. I have to put them at the bottom of the pile so that I'm not using the same three plates over and over again. It's the same for the silverware. I put the ones that are cleanly washed underneath so the old ones come up to the top. I suppose that way they don't feel that I'm ignoring some of them!

Administrator, television, male, 29

I eat everything on my plate in order of preference, starting with the one I like the least, and finishing with what I like best. Also, I completely finish one item before continuing on to the next. So, if there are two vegetables and meat on the plate, I'll eat one vegetable, then the other vegetable and then the meat, my favorite, last.

Dental technician, male, 55

I eat five or six bananas every day on my way to work in a three-piece suit.

HIS GIRLFRIEND: He places the peels in a bag and just keeps eating them. If he can't get them in one shop, he goes to another shop along his route until he finds them.

Banker, male, 26
His girlfriend is a graduate student, 24

My brother peels everything from a tomato to a grape. He won't eat them otherwise.

Sales engineer, male, 53
His brother is a businessman, 47

Any container that I can open in a supermarket, I do. Mostly ice cream, sour cream and cottage cheese. Cottage cheese has to have the right consistency and wateryness otherwise it clumps in your mouth. Sometimes I have to check a few of them to get the right one.

Teacher, photography, female, 35

My life is spent at lunch with clients and I'm supposed to act extremely sophisticated. Unfortunately, I have two obnoxious habits which I do without thinking, even in the most elegant restaurants. One is crunching ice. When you order a spritzer with presidents and vice presidents of client companies, one should not sit there and crunch ice. Crunching ice is bad enough but the other thing I generally do, again without thinking, is chew straws until I absolutely mangle them.

Account executive, ad agency, male, 29

When a friend of mine eats meat and potatoes and peas, she has one pea with every forkful of potatoes and meat. If she runs out of peas, she won't finish her meal.

Housewife, early fifties
Her friend is a real estate agent, female, 51

Before I eat, I rub my belly in a rotating manner and when I'm done eating, I do the same thing. It helps the digestive processes and makes me feel better.

Physician, male, 36

When I'm talking to people, especially in a restaurant, I have to keep my hands busy. I find myself taking whatever is at hand and stripping it down or playing with it, like the label on a bottle of beer or wax on a paper cup. If there's nothing there, I'll pour a little bit of the salt out and play with that but I usually find something. It'll be a slow progression as I'm talking. The other person may be smoking, I'll be tearing a napkin or crushing a soda can.

Fudge maker, male, 37

I absolutely cannot eat a Bavarian cream puff without saying "Mmmmmmmmmmmmmm Mmmmmmmmmmmmmmm San Antone!" I've tried not to but the minute I put a bite in my mouth, I hear myself saying, "Mmmmmmmmmmmmmm Mmmmmmmmmmmmmmm San Antone!" It's physically impossible not to!

Illustrator, male, 42

I eat everything on my plate . . . the meat, the potatoes, the vegetables, and sometimes the salad, evenly, in rotation, so I'm finished with everything at the same time.

Vice President, television network, male, 49

I'd rather buy someone a whole soda or ice cream cone of their own than give them the smallest taste of mine. It's got nothing to do with germs. I just enjoy something a lot more when I eat the whole thing. Maybe it's because I eat a lot and if I don't drink or eat the whole thing, I don't feel like I'm quenching my thirst or satisfying my appetite.

Student, male, 19

On Monday nights, I have a card game and there's no time to cook or eat out. I have an arrangement with the owner of a deli to hold a porterhouse steak for me which he double-wraps in aluminum foil. I place it on the block where the carburetor is, there's a spot there where it won't fall out and by the time I get to my card game, it's perfectly done on both sides and I have a delicious dinner.

Photographer, male, 43

I like to make dirty words with the letters in Campbell's Soup. Sometimes I put them on a cracker. I can't say them in public and it gives me a kick to do it through my soup.

Accountant, male, 22

I'm a club soda freak. I drink lots of it but I won't drink out of the same bottle twice, even if all I had was a sip. I'll open a fresh one and throw the other one away. I like the fizzy sound when I open it up.

Manufacturer, printing ink, male, late forties

When I go away for a weekend, I completely pig out. So Sunday night, when I get home, I take a couple of laxatives to lose the weight I gained.

Media buyer, female, "thirtyish"

When I'm home, I will only drink coffee out of one particular cup. It's white with red stripes. I'll drink other liquids out of the other cups, but not coffee. It must be that cup and no other. If it's dirty, I'll go wash it even if there are several other clean ones on the shelf.

Serigrapher, female, 23

When I eat corn on the cob, I eat it row by row, all the way across, left to right and all the way around, very neatly. Just like a typewriter. It drives me crazy when the kids take random bites.

Secretary, female, 33

I never pass a water fountain without stopping to take a drink. It stimulates me.

Retired, male, 41

I know it's silly because they don't taste any different, but I separate my M&M's by color before I eat them. I save the green M&M's for last because those are the prettiest. I eat the brown ones first because I like those the least, then the light browns. I get rid of the oranges next, then the yellows, and then the greens.

Financial analyst, female, 32

The meat and the vegetables must be in separate dishes because I can't stand the thought of the juices running into each other.

Teacher, junior high school, female, 26

queasy cuisine

My mother always got involved in some very strange sandwiches. First, because she's from the deep South and second, because she grew up during the depression. She's been known to eat pineapple and mayonnaise sandwiches, usually on white bread. And often she'll take a can of Campbell's bean soup and spread it on bread and eat that as a sandwich.

Marketing consultant, female, 33
Her mother is a housewife, 54

I like to eat condiments—soy sauce, mayonnaise, mustard, tartar sauce, salad dressing. I'll go in the refrigerator with a spoon and eat a little bit of each one.

Financial analyst, female, 25

When I eat any kind of sandwich, I put mayonnaise on one side and mustard on the other.

Hack driver, owns horse and carriage, male, 24

I eat potato chip sandwiches. Potato chips on white bread. I don't put anything else on it. It's a very simple sandwich and it's delicious! When I'm really hungry, that's what I think about.

Hair colorist, male, "Don't ask my age, I'll have a nervous breakdown."

I love mayonnaise sandwiches on white bread at any time.

Pharmacist, male, 31

I chew on chicken bones to make myself feel like I've eaten something when I haven't. I enjoy chewing on them. In fact, I usually take the meat off the bones and eat the bones.

Teacher, remedial math, female, 29

My brother's favorite food to eat in the whole world is sweet pickles and peanut butter on white bread. The thought of it makes me sick. And I really can't understand it because he's a gourmet cook and a very finicky eater. But he just loves it and he's been eating it for years.

Assisant account executive, female, 21
Her brother is a student, 17

I always order apple pie because I love apple pie but I hate apples so I only eat the crust.

Attorney, male, 36

I always drink Tab first thing in the morning because I'm too hot to drink coffee. Water just doesn't make it. I like the fizziness in my mouth.

Writer/producer, female, 27

When I drink tea, the milk has to be in the cup first, otherwise I don't want it. My mother always did it that way.

Secretary, female, "over 40"

I bring lots of food with me to the movies because the minute I sit down, I get hungry. I prefer sandwiches or chicken to popcorn or candy. It makes the movie more enjoyable. I bring some wet paper towels with me so I can wipe my hands.

Maid, female, 60

I used to work for a real character who ate the exact same lunch every single day of his life—liverwurst on rye. And every day he would comment, "The liverwurst is so thin, you can read a newspaper through it."

Commercial photographer, male, 48
His former employer is a retired art dealer,
male, seventies

I take vitamins by increasing size to prepare my throat for the larger size.

Investigator, insurance company, male, 32

I line up the vitamin bottles on the kitchen counter from the tallest to the smallest. I take them in that sequence, the largest on down.

Hairstylist, male, 35

I've never had an olive in my life. I won't eat it because it smells. I've never tasted beer for the same reason.

ME: And you're not curious about how it tastes?

On, no. Not at all. I won't eat oysters or snails either. I have a closed palate. I'm not adventurous about food.

Nurse, female, 32

I take a lot of vitamins in the morning but I always have them in alphabetical order according to the letter of the vitamin. I'll have Vitamin B-1 before I'll have Vitamin C which I'll have before Vitamin D which I'll have before Vitamin E which I'll have before the multiple.

Writer, television, male, 28

My wife is an exceptionally neat eater. When she eats mashed potatoes, she will take her knife, and/or fork and pat it into a neat arrangement, almost symmetrical, flatten it out, and then eat it section by section. She will continue to keep it uniform after she removes a portion of it by flattening it in place again. Flat and neat!

President, typesetting company, male, 36
His wife is a housewife, 35

I must keep going back to a restaurant until I've sampled everything on the menu at least once. To break the monotony, I do three or four restaurants at one time. Then I'll start going to a different one.

Sales agent, accessories, male, 46

My father eats a banana sideways, like corn on the cob. He eats them in sections.

HER FATHER: There are four natural sections to a banana, four major breaking points and I try to eat it by each individual section.

Student, female, 20
Her father is a manufacturer's representative, 49

I cut my spaghetti with a knife and fork in neat bite-size chunks. I start at the front of the plate and work my way to the back. I don't like to deal with the winding.

HIS WIFE: He even did it in Italy and offended a lot of Italians!

House painter, male, 38

Every couple of weeks, I cook dinner in my dishwasher. I put potatoes, onions, carrots, a piece of fish or little pieces of beef and about two inches of water in a large pot with a screw-on lid. I put it in the dishwasher, run it through the cycle, without soap, of course, and it steams the whole thing. I have a perfect meal when I take it out.

Photographer, male, 43

It's so much easier and faster to drink right out of the bottle. I can't be bothered with pouring it into a glass and then having to wash the glass. If there are people around, I turn away so they can't see me.

Marriage counselor, female, 27

My cousin hums and shakes his leg when he eats. It doesn't sound like anything I've ever heard. He does it in restaurants, anywhere. We don't see him too often as a result.

Owner, retail cleaning business, male, 39
His cousin is a teacher, science, male, 41

I never put my coffee cup back in the saucer after I take the first sip. I tend to put it on the counter or table. A friend of mine pointed this out to me about six years ago. I never realized it until then.

Physician, male, 35

I eat my pie continental style. Instead of eating from the point to the back, I start from the back where the crust is and work my way forward. I like the taste of the crust first instead of leaving it for last.

Advertising coordinator, male, 23

I have a habit of eating my desserts first because it's the best part of the meal. I don't want the restaurant to run out of my favorite dessert or my stomach to run out of room.

Secretary, female, would not give age

I always peel a banana very well, taking all the little skins off. Then I put it under running cold water and dry if off before I eat it. I'm not a clean nut, it has nothing to do with germs. It just seems to taste fresher somehow.

Executive secretary, female, 33

When I eat my cereal, I prefer not to see the tablespoon full of milk. I pour the milk off each spoonful, eat the cereal, and at the end I'm left with a bowl of milk.

Architect, male, 29

I always drink coffee or tea out of a stemmed glass. I don't like it out of a cup. No matter how highly glazed it is, china or porcelain is still porous and absorbs a little of whatever was left in it last, no matter how much you wash it.

Assistant television producer, male, 36

My baked potatoes must be cut across the short side, not lengthwise. It drives me crazy if it isn't!

Product manager, marketing, female, "over 30"

I take all the pits out of watermelons before I start eating it so I don't have to worry about them. Some of the pits are deeply embedded in the watermelon and major surgery is required to remove them. An ordinary kitchen knife wastes too much of the watermelon. I have found that by far the most efficient utensil for this purpose is a pointed dart.

Lawyer, male, 34

Anytime I have a cup of coffee, I immediately light a cigarette. If I don't have any cigarettes, I'll ignore the coffee or do without it.

Associate director, television, male, 33

My grandmother used to put orange juice on her cereal and when we asked her why she did it, she said it didn't matter, she couldn't taste it anyhow! She was 80.

Textile wholesaler, male, 33

I take the kernels of corn off the cob with a fork as opposed to eating it right off the cob. It's neater and more convenient than biting it off. I once saw an uncle of mine do it who had trouble with false teeth and I thought it was a fabulous idea.

Production manager, printing company, male, 44

We have plenty of regular cups and glasses but I've adopted a little fruit jar as my water glass. This quirk originated in the Navy and it just stuck with me.

Maintenance man, 60

When there's a waiting list in restaurants, I like to give them a phony name just for the hell of it. It amuses me. If I feel particularly cocky, I tell them my name is Party. It's funny to hear the hostess say, "Will the party of Party follow me please." Sometimes I say I'm Dr. So and So. I usually get a better table and service.

Manufacturer, plastics, male, 38

Most people hold the knife in their right hand and the fork in the left. I do the reverse and always have. I hold the fork in my right hand and the knife in my left and I eat in this fashion, although I'm right-handed.

Artist, male, 32

If I'm having dessert with a cup of coffee, I'll put Sweet'N Lo in the coffee. Psychologically, I think I'm losing weight by saving calories even though I may be having a very caloric piece of pie.

Executive, male, 28

I can't eat food that's two different textures. For instance, I can't eat a tomato because it's hard on the outside and squishy on the inside. It gives me a violent reaction. You bite through the hard part and it squishes all over the inside of your mouth and to me, that's disgusting.

Graduate student, male, 26

I eat the bun and throw the hamburger away. I don't like the idea of eating meat but I like the flavor. So when I go to Burger King or one of those places, I order the hamburger but all I eat is the lettuce and tomato and the bread which has the flavor of the meat in it. I do the same with apples. I eat the peel, which has more vitamins anyway, and throw the apple away. I always pick out the best parts of food when I'm eating and throw the rest away. That's the way I am with life. I feel a little uncomfortable about doing it in public but I have friends now who just accept it as part of me so it's no big deal anymore.

Manager, boutique, female, 22

I keep important papers and documents, like my dissertation, in the vegetable compartment of the refrigerator because it's the most fireproof place in my apartment.

Anthropologist, female, 31

When I open up a half gallon of ice cream, I eat right out of the container and very evenly, very neatly level off each layer as I eat it. I start around the edges because it's softer and I keep leveling off the ice cream as I go down, until I finish it.

Graphic designer, male, 33

My father has to end a meal with one bite of each item on his plate. If any of the items are not completely finished, he leaves it over. He calls it a "balanced meal."

Stylist, female, 23
Her father is an architect, 54

SCORE:

Just for the fun of it, if you want to know how your eating oddities rate next to other people's, use this as a guide:

Under fifteen similar—You're only a moderately interesting dinner guest.

From fifteen to twenty-five—You're probably a riot at smorgasbords where there are so many different kinds of food to have fetishes about.

More than twenty-five—You qualify for the coveted Julia Child Culinary Quirk Award.

Bedtime stories you haven't heard before!

Your mom and dad think it's cute that you sleep with a 100-watt night light because you're afraid of the dark. It's a perfectly reasonable quirk. (Don't let the fact that you're a forty-three-year-old well-respected politician and the father of three children disturb you.)

You have an overwhelming but unconscious need to steal the blanket off your mate in the middle of the night and completely wind yourself up in it so he can't pull any back.

You're an attractive, intelligent male who has no problem meeting women. Holding on to them, literally and otherwise, seems to be a problem, however, because they just don't enjoy sleeping under the bed as much as you.

You find that television has a strange effect on you. It puts you to sleep. At 10 P.M., your children are wondering where you are.

You sleep completely naked except for those red ear muffs. It's not that you're into skiing and want to be ready when it snows. It's just that, somehow, your blood turns to water when it's circulating through your ears and they're extremely sensitive to cold air. We understand.

What do the above people have in common? They are:

A. Part of the Hare Krishna cult.

B.   Out-patients at Bellevue Psychiatric Ward.
C.   Members of Studio 54.
D.   Normal people.
E.   All the same person. You described me to a tee.

Wrong, they're normal people. So don't get insomnia worrying about your quirks. It's amazing what we take to bed with us. Rituals—I mean, really, you know you set the alarm. Why get up again to check it. Dozens of pillows—three under your head, two over your head, one to hug, four to line up next to you. Stuffed animals. Live animals. And wait till you read what else. What type of sleeper are you?

I name my pillows. One is Susan Saint James and the other one is Racquel Welch.

ME: What do you do with your pillows?

I just hold them closely and dream on those long, cold nights in New York City when I don't have female companionship.

Assistant marketing manager, male, 29

I hate to admit this. It probably stems from my childhood. For a long time, I'd glance under the bed before I got in to make sure no one was there. I don't think I do it anymore. Anyway, I wouldn't admit it if I did.

Business executive, male, 45

When I wake up in the morning, I start counting to one hundred and tell myself that when I get to one hundred, I'll get up. I always think I counted too quickly and start over. I go through this about five or six times before I actually get up.

Management consultant, male, 33

Although I take a shower at night, I wash my feet again in the sink right before I go to bed. It makes me feel refreshed.

Housewife, 32

Every man likes to sleep on a particular side of the bed. Some time ago, my wife came to me and said that she read in a magazine that if she continued to sleep on her side of the bed, she'd develop facial wrinkles. I was given the choice of allowing that to happen to her by being stubborn about my side of the bed or moving. I'm now sleeping on the wrong side of the bed. And I think I'm getting wrinkles.

Family therapist, male, 52
His wife is a vice president, phone equipment
company, 46

My grandmother puts a large sheet of plastic over her pillows and headboard to protect them from scalp grease. And she sleeps on the plastic.

Student, female, 23
Her grandmother is an artist, 78

About twenty-five minutes after I've gotten into bed, I'll wake up and think, 'I forgot to set the alarm.' I check it and, of course it's okay, so I get back into bed. In another twenty-five minutes, I wake up thinking the same thing. I go through this ritual two or three times a night before I actually believe I've set it.

Fashion buyer, female, 30

For all my life, at least from my earliest recollection, it's been physically impossible for me to fall asleep without my navel being covered. If it's summer and I'm naked, I still have to have a part of the sheet come across my navel or I can't sleep. When I'm wearing underpants, sometimes I'll be suddenly aware that something is wrong . . . the waistband of my underpants is too low. When I realize it, I pull the waistband over my navel and then I can go to sleep.

Photographer, male, 28

I always sleep with the light on. The brighter, the better. I don't like the dark. Besides sleeping with the light on, I must make love with the light on. To me it's more terrific.

Crafts designer/author, female, 30

For five years, my bed was perpendicular to the wall. Now my apartment is being redone and the bed has been built into a platform and it is now parallel to the wall. I still sleep perpendicular to the wall across the short side of the bed. It creates too much confusion within my body to adjust to the new direction so I let my feet hang over.

Partner, commodity brokerage firm, male, 30

I have to sleep with my socks on, preferably tennis socks because they keep my feet warm. That's all I wear. In the summer the air-conditioning is going so I still need to have my feet warm.

Manager, computer center, male, 35

I must wash my face before I go to sleep even if I've washed it a half hour earlier. Otherwise I can't fall asleep. If I get into bed without washing my face, I'll toss and turn until I finally get up and wash my face. When I get back into bed, I fall asleep immediately.

Accountant, female, 43

My sheets must be 100% cotton and they must have at least 180 threads per inch. There's only one brand of all-cotton sheets that are still made and they have 200 threads per inch. Other sheets give me abrasions.

Attorney, male, 34

I have difficulty going to sleep at night unless I have an extra blanket wrapped around my head covering my eyes. It's a special all-cotton, full-size thermal blanket. I don't use a pillow. I just wad up the extra part and use that as a pillow. If I visit people and I miss my blanket, I borrow a large towel.

Attorney, female, 33

I have a full bed but in order to fall asleep I have to be on the right side. If I'm in the middle or the left, I'll toss and turn and stay awake. The only way I can go to sleep is if I sleep on the right-hand side.

Advertising coordinator, female, 28

I never, ever sleep on the right side of the bed. It's always the left side—I don't care if I'm alone or with somebody, it's still the left side, always.

ME: Why?

I just feel more comfortable.

ME: Are you right-handed or left-handed?

Right-handed.

Musician, male, 37

When I sleep with a date, I prefer to sleep on the right side. When I sleep alone, I prefer to sleep in the middle.

Attorney, male, 45

Every night, before I go to sleep, I have to know whether the Red Sox won. In fact, I won't go to sleep unless I find out the final scores. Luckily, there's a sports recording you can call in New York which reports the updated scores every fifteen minutes.

Graduate student, male, 26

I usually sleep on my back and put the edge of the sheet between my teeth. I don't know how it started. I've tried to analyze it and decided that the worst thing that can happen is that I'll chew a hole in the sheet!

Art director, male, 45

My feet or arms cannot hang over the edge of the bed because the monsters under the bed will get them. Sometimes, I have to take a running leap from the door of the bedroom to the bed because they'll get me while I'm standing there. Many times, in the middle of the night, my leg or arm will sort of fall out and I'll immediately feel it and I'll think, "This is ridiculous, I'm thirty-two years old, there aren't any monsters under the bed!" but I have to do it or else I can't go back to sleep again!

Special assistant to director, museum, female, 32

I only wear long, white nightgowns. It really bothers me to think of wearing any other color because it doesn't feel clean enough. I once had to buy a green one in an emergency because the store was out of white ones and I don't sleep well when I'm wearing it. Sheets and pillow cases can be colored although my mother only uses white bedding and that always seems the absolute cleanest. It's one of the pleasures of going home and sleeping— white nightgown, white bed.

Junior account executive, female, 21

The television set must be on when I go to sleep and it burns all night long. I shut it off when I wake up in the morning. I've tried to go to sleep without it, no can do!

Retail butcher, male, 40

I check every bed that's not my own, in a hotel, or motel, to make sure it's not short-sheeted. If it is, I have to remake the bed, because I don't want my body to touch the mattress. Most beds are short-sheeted so you can imagine how many beds I have to remake! It was not a hit on my honeymoon!

Secretary, female, 48

I put my underwear under my pillow when I go to sleep. I was never consciously aware that I did this, it's second nature by now, until my wife pointed it out to me one day. She asked me why I did it so I started thinking about it. Why do I do it? It certainly doesn't accomplish anything. As I thought about it, I realized that I wasn't entirely crazy—there was a perfectly valid reason for it. It started when I was in a forced labor camp in Hungary during the war. When I got undressed to prepare to go to sleep, I put my clothing in a pile. By morning, I would discover that someone who obviously didn't have a pair, had stolen my underwear. After this incident, I began placing them under a makeshift pillow. I got so used to doing this that I just continued the habit after the war. It's still a part of my bedtime routine although my wife has sworn she won't steal them!

Dental instrument mechanic, male, 64

If my right thigh should touch my left thigh, I would immediately wake up. I can't fall asleep if they're making any contact so I use the blanket to separate my legs. Someone else's skin touching mine doesn't bother me, just my own. I guess I must be allergic to myself.

Printer, male, 40

I have to have a glass of ice water at my nightstand every night by eleven-twenty, with three cubes of ice. I can't go to sleep without it. It is a glass I do not drink from. If I want water, I go to the kitchen, even if it's the middle of the night.

Receptionist, female, 21

74

The opening of my pillow case has to be to my right when I'm lying on my back. Always—no matter where I am.

Writer/producer, female, 33

Before I go to sleep, I always put a glass of juice on my night table. I rarely drink it but it must be there in case I get thirsty in the middle of the night.

Seamstress, 66

I must have a tissue in my hand when I go to bed in case I have to blow my nose in the middle of the night. If a facial tissue is unavailable, I'll use a piece of toilet paper or a napkin. I hold it as I fall asleep. And if I wake up during the night, I look for it or take another one if I can't find it because I usually let go of it at some point. There are always tissues tucked around my bed.

Manager, pre-school, female, 30

All my life I slept on my stomach until I had an ulcer operation and I was forced to sleep on my back. I resolved the situation by placing the pillow on my stomach which made me feel like I was sleeping on my stomach and since then I always sleep that way.

Owner, clothing boutique, male, 32

I do some wild, neurotic things that I think are normal. In a conjugal bed, when she wants to cuddle, I really can't get into it because I have to be hanging off the edge of the bed and if she starts to cuddle, I'll wind up kissing the rug. I just can't sleep in the middle of beds. A piece of my body has to be touching the edge. It's just more comfortable that way. I get some strange reactions and questions from pseudo-psychologists who try to figure it out like, "Whatever happened to you when you were a child?"

Account executive, ad agency, male, 29

I'm terrified of flies landing on my body when I sleep so I have to be completely covered for that reason. Flies are so filthy and I'm a bit of a clean-freak.

Student, female, 33

I cannot go to sleep at home or in a hotel room or in someone else's home, without first totally pulling the bedspread and all covers and sheets out from being tucked in so that everything lies loosely and free and unconfined.

Copywriter, female, 30

I sleep very comfortably as long as I have a pillow to put over my eyes to keep any light out. I sleep with two pillows and I like room darkeners and drapes. I don't like any light whatsoever in the bedroom. As a matter of fact, if somebody would light a match, it would wake me up.

Dentist, male, 45

I won't sleep on sheets that have holes in them. I don't care about the pillow cases or the blanket, just the sheets. I have been known to check into a motel room and spend the first five minutes or so inspecting the sheets to make sure there are no holes in them. This leads to some very strange reactions indeed from my companions who look at me as if I'm crazy, which I probably am. In fact, when my ex-wife and I first went away for a weekend, and I went through my sheet-check routine, it was almost the first and last time we went away. Perhaps, in hindsight, it might have been a better thing. My therapist can't figure it out either.

Lawyer, male, 36

I must have sex every day at 6:15 P.M., after the sun goes down and before the moon comes up. That's when I enjoy it most. For me, it's like brushing my teeth, it's a must. I've buried a few husbands, I'm on my third marriage.

Housewife, fifties

Unless I have my two pigs, I can't go to sleep at night. One is gray and female and the other one is pink and male. They're stuffed animals. I use them to prop up my elbow and knee and when I'm away from home I have to substitute with pillows but it's just not the same.

Film maker, female, 28

Every night when I go to bed, I wipe my feet off before I get in, even if I've worn socks and my feet are perfectly clean. I sit down on the bed, grab each foot by the ankle and wipe it off with my hand.

Cabana boy, male, 21

I like to sleep high, so I use three pillows all the time. Without them, forget it, I can't fall asleep. I always ask for more pillows in a hotel.

Chauffeur, male, 51

I have a fear of not getting up in the morning, so I set two alarm clocks. If one doesn't go off, the other one will.

Statistician, female, 35

When I sleep in the nude, I put a pair of undershorts near the bed. If there's a fire in the middle of the night, I want to be able to run outside with something on!

Textile wholesaler, male, 33

When I was in college and lived in the dorm, I wanted to have all my valuables nearby when I was sleeping. So, before going to bed, I'd put my wallet, my watch, my keys and any change in my shoes. It seemed reasonable at the time except, now, seventeen years later, I still do it.

Owner, marketing sales promotion company, male, 38

I sleep on a bare mattress so I don't have to wash the sheets.

Consultant, labor relations, male, 27

It's very difficult for me to make love to a woman unless she's on my right. It just feels so much better and more comfortable when I'm on the left.

Sound engineer, male, 33

A friend of mine has to make the bed instantly as soon as she and her husband wake up. One Sunday her husband got up to go to the bathroom, and by the time he came back, the bed was made.

Teacher, handicapped children, female, 32
Her friend is a stock reporter, 38

Quite often I wake my husband up at around 2:00 A.M. to let him know that our sons are not at home and I'm concerned. I then turn over and go back to sleep while he spends the rest of the morning hours up, waiting for them to come home. As long as he's doing my worrying for me, I can relax.

Jeweler, female, 44

My friend and his wife usually sleep head to head but during a full moon he sleeps head to foot because he's afraid he'll wake up in the middle of the night and bite her neck.

Manager, retail store, male, 32
His friend is a vice president, bank, male, 35

No matter how great a party we've been to or how extensive a dinner we've had, my husband and I must have a bowl of cereal right before we go to sleep. If I don't have the cereal, I will think I'm famished and simply cannot get through the night.

Housewife, 60
Her husband is an engineer, 65

I like very smooth, soft pillow cases and I bring my own with me on all my trips. I use either the satin acetate kind or very old ones that are almost tearing so they're soft. Whenever I can, if I'm not going to Europe, and the weight of the luggage doesn't matter, I like to bring my own pillow as well, because the only kind I can sleep on is foam rubber.

Textile designer, female, 34

My wife, Elenore, has a special pillow that goes with her wherever she goes. It's been all over the world. She can't sleep on a strange pillow.

Merchandising manager, produce, male, 47
Elenore is a housewife, 47

No matter where I am or which side of the bed I'm on, I have to turn my back to the middle in order to fall asleep.

Manufacturer, neckwear, male, 28

I admire the view from our bedroom window of the Manhattan skyline and every night before I go to sleep, I say goodnight to the Empire State Building.

HIS WIFE: When he's out of town, I do it for him. I say, "Goodnight from Marshall," with my eyes focused on the Empire State Building.

Computer consultant, male, 36
His wife is a student, 33

I don't like going to bed and for all intensive purposes, waking up the next second and having eight to twelve hours of my life disappear. I like to experience those hours so I get up several times during the night. I like the quiet and the solitude. I also enjoy languishing in bed and the experience of going back to sleep.

Gemologist, male, 27

I lie on my stomach and kick my feet up and down as though I were swimming to fall asleep. It relieves tension.

Theatrical agent, female, 39

After my boyfriend and I make love, he gets up and waters the plants. Sometimes it gives him energy and instead of just cooling out, he waters the plants. We have about a hundred of them.

Program auditor, female, 22
Her boyfriend is a Harvard MBA candidate

I sleep with four pillows lined up alongside myself. I make believe it's another body next to me.

Salesman, insurance, 44

When the lights are off and my husband is just about to drowse off, he'll knock twice on the headboard to keep evil spirits away. He's been doing this since childhood.

Housewife, 39
Her husband is an executive, 44

My particular quirk developed when I was in the Navy. When the ships used to rock, I'd feel very uncomfortable and unstable. I was always afraid I would fall off the bed which was a cot at the time. So I developed the habit of putting one foot on the floor to fall asleep. I've been out of the service for many years but to this day, I have to sleep with one leg on the floor. I've been married a couple of times and my wives have thought this to be highly unusual. But it works.

Television producer, male, 39

Ever since I traveled around Europe as a student eight years ago, I've slept with my watch on. At the time, we stayed in hostels and hotels and I didn't want it to get stolen. Later I saw Jean-Paul Belmondo in a movie and he always kept his watch on so that reinforced my quirk.

Account executive, ad agency, male, 29

When my grandmother goes to sleep, she points one shoe forward and the other one in the opposite direction so no one can step into them at night. She's Italian.

Sales manager, male, 35
His grandmother is 79

I fold my pillow and lie down with my head in a certain position so the pillow doesn't move because I don't want my hair to be out of place when I wake up in the morning.

Executive, garment center, male, 41

I have to be covered with a sheet up to my neck, no matter how hot it is. And it has to be tucked underneath my feet, otherwise I can't sleep.

Purchasing agent, female, 32

I sleep on my back and pull the sheet up so it covers my mouth. I have no idea why I do this.

Seamstress, 66

In order to fall asleep, I must be lying so that my head is pointed toward the west and my feet to the east. Otherwise I just can't sleep. I was once in a hotel on vacation and I had a very difficult time falling asleep, until I finally realized what the problem was, and turned the bed in the proper direction. I immediately fell asleep. Since then, I always take a compass with me when I travel. As soon as I arrive in my room, I arrange the bed so that it's lined up east and west.

Dental instrument mechanic, male, 64

When my mate and I go to bed every evening, he gets into bed with his undershorts, and I take them off. It has nothing to do with sex. He doesn't do the same for me because I go to bed nude.

Social worker, female, 33

Every night before I go to sleep, no matter where I am, I try to have milk and cookies, or milk and a cupcake. If, for some reason, I can't have it, I'm grouchy, and don't feel satisfied and can't fall asleep right away. If I run out, I'll go out in the middle of the night and drive as far as a mile to get some.

Cab owner/driver, male, 30

I'm always very happy when I wake up. I don't think in my whole life, I have ever, except for about ten times, gotten up in a bad mood. Things may happen during the course of the day to put me in a bad mood but I always wake up feeling great.

Owner, furniture store, female, 32

I make my bed when I get home at night even if it's fifteen minutes before I go to sleep. I have to get into a neat bed but I can't be bothered with making it in the morning. Sometimes I'll get home at eleven o'clock, make the bed, then unmake it, get in and go to sleep.

Attorney, male, 26

Anything I do or come into contact with at night, right before I go to bed, I must do or touch three times. I check the locks on the door, and actually lock and unlock them three times. My alarm clock is set for seven o'clock but I go around and re-set it three times. I turn the alarm on and off and make sure it rings three times. I brush my teeth three times. I rinse my face three times. I flip my pillow over three times. When I was small, I used to watch my father play cards. He would walk around his chair three times for good luck to win the game and that's probably where it originated. Three's the magic number!

Housewife, 28

I sleep in the nude with the window open and don't use a blanket no matter what the weather is.

Security guard, male, 34

I have to check the entire house to make sure that all the drawers, closets and windows are shut tight before I go to sleep, regardless of how tired I may be. If it's open just a hair, I won't be able to sleep.

Fashion buyer, female, 30

I roll my pillow up in a certain position and give it a karate chop. Then I stick it under my neck. I don't sleep with my head on the pillow.

Owner, warehousing business, male, 44

I suffer from a chronic "Hot Feet" condition which requires me to have my feet outside the covers at all times regardless of the temperature. Until about a month ago, I was convinced that monsters were circulating in my room ready to kill me during the night, probably for good reason. The monsters and I had a pact, however, that they would not attack my feet. They could attack any other part of me but they would leave my feet alone and that way we would get along.

Development coordinator, public TV station, male, 22

I must wear a fresh, clean nightgown every night. If I'm on vacation and I run out of clean ones, I'll keep washing the one I have even if I've only worn it once.

Housewife, female, 58

I'm most comfortable when one leg is underneath the blanket and the other leg is on top. When I turn around, the leg that was under goes over, and the other leg is under.

Art director, male, 45

I always sleep with my right hand flat against the wall over my head. It doesn't matter in what position I fall asleep, I still hold the wall. I like a lot of blankets but I also like to be cool when I sleep and touching a cold wall helps to cool me down.

Marketing manager, cosmetics company,
female, 24

Every night, before we go to sleep, my husband and I simultaneously say a four-line poem that his mother used to say to him as a child. And occasionally, when we're apart, I say it anyway. It goes like this:
    Goodnight.
    Sleep tight.
    Pleasant dreams.
    See you in the morning.

Writer, female, 27
Her husband is a banker, 27

SCORE:

Come out from under the covers and fess up.

If you recognize yourself among those listed in this chapter six times or less—Go back to sleep.

Seven to seventeen times—You think you're normal? Dream on.

Over eighteen times—Take two aspirin, drink liquids and get plenty of rest. Good luck.

Clothes encounters of the strange kind

Who's to tell you how to dress or undress. You've never seen Bella Abzug without her hat, Johnny Carson always wears non-matching cufflinks and Woody Allen likes to wear sneakers with his tux, so you're in good company.

Clothes mean different things to different people. To my friend Bubbles LaRose, they mean absolutely nothing. But for the rest of us, it's time to come out of the closet. You macho guys out there with one earring, are you listening? As for some of you ladies, if God wanted you to have four earrings in each ear lobe and one in your right nostril, he would have put more holes in your head. If you want to wear your shirt unbuttoned to your navel with lots of gold chains, suit yourself. If status initials are your bag, Louis Vuitton loves people like you. So does Gucci. They're cashing in on your quirk right this minute. The worst thing that can happen to you if you're a Sock, Shoe, Sock, Shoe Person as opposed to a Sock, Sock, Shoe, Shoe Person is that you'll hop out of your apartment if there's a fire. And if you're a Tall Blond Man with One Black Shoe and One Brown Shoe and it happens regularly, even on Daylight Savings mornings when you don't have a hangover, you certainly qualify.

Have you ever wondered why some joggers wear their shorts over their sweat pants? It doesn't make them run faster and it doesn't make them look better, so it must be a quirk that started because the elastic in some schnook's pants was all stretched out and he wore his shorts to hold them up. Because it was the beginning of the jogging rage, everyone assumed, "Hey, this guy knows what he's doing. I should dress like that if I want to look like a pro." And, thus, the beginning of a quirk that probably got around faster than he did.

It won't be the same looking at the world through hot-pink, glittered Fiorucci fifties glasses, if that's your schtick, and believe me, the world won't look at you the same either.

Tomorrow morning concentrate on which leg you put in your pants or panty hose first, then try to do it the other way. Then come up with a good excuse explaining to your boss why you were late. Some people put both legs in their pants at the same time. They're unbalanced people.

It doesn't matter what your hang-ups are in clothes. Unless, of course, you wear a raincoat. And nothing else. And flash. Then, I'd say, you've got a problem.

Just remember that it's not whether you put your underwear on first or last that counts. It's whether they're clean . . . in case you get into an accident.

———

When I put my pantyhose on, I always put my right leg in first. I've tried to do it the other way, but I have to take it off, and do it again.

ME: Why?

If I knew why, it wouldn't be a quirk!

Fund raiser, female, would not give age

I don't use an ironing board even if there's one in the house. It's so much easier to put a towel on the bed and iron on the bed, especially since I iron my clothes the day I'm going to wear them, not all at the same time.

Administrative assistant, female, 24

I like to line up my shoes under the bed, like soldiers. I have about a dozen pairs under there. My wife thinks I'm nuts. They're easier to get on this way—I just step out of bed and put on my shoes! Otherwise, I'd have to go to the closet.

Retoucher, male, 58

The laces in my shoes have to have equal tension. If one shoe-lace is looser than the other, I have to stop and re-tie both so the pressure is exactly the same.

Estimator, media department, ad agency,
female, 22

My grandmother, who was in the jewelry business, taught me never to wear white gold or silver with yellow gold. She felt it wasn't right to mix the two so I never do.

Marketing consultant, female, 33

It drives me nuts to see people walking around with their pocket flaps in or their collar up. I have to go over and say, "Why don't you fix your pocket flaps, you'll get wrinkles." They do adjust their pocket or collar but their expression says, "Who are you? What do you care?"

Retoucher, male, 26

When I want to remind myself about something, I turn my watch around and wear it with the dial underneath. It's so uncomfortable that I always remember what I have to do.

Waiter, male, 33

I like my clothes completely wrinkled. I hate creases. I hate anything brand new. In fact, I scuff up a new pair of shoes before I wear them. I'll walk through mud, get them wet, walk on the sides of them. If it's already wrinkled, I don't have to worry about getting it wrinkled. I'm more comfortable and relaxed.

Model, male, 35

When someone with a hat is walking down the street in front of me, I have this overwhelming urge to flip the hat off. Luckily, I've managed to keep this feeling under control but I think it would be fun to follow through one of these days.

Illustrator, male, 23

A lot of people are fascinated by the fact that I wear a white sock on my left foot and another color, which changes from day to day, on my right foot. I like to be unique.

Manufacturer, ladies' apparel, male, 44

My friend hangs all her clothing up inside out. She's really compulsive about it. She will very carefully, very neatly, turn all her dresses, skirts, pants and blouses inside out, button or zip them and hang them on hangers that way. She's not quite clear herself about why she does this. She says it's probably because they stay cleaner.

Assistant account executive, female, 21
Her friend is a girl friday, 22

My sister wears the same pair of socks to her shrink every week. They make her feel comfortable.

Actress, 32
Her sister is a teacher, 42

I change my underwear at least three times a day. In the morning, when I come home from work and before I go to bed. It's a hygienic thing. Some people have to wash their hands eight hundred times a day, I just change my underwear.

Account executive, public relations, female, 27

I put on a different cologne every day of the week. I don't like to smell the same odors on myself consistently. If I was particularly lucky one day, I'll wear the same cologne to bring me luck again when I feel I need it.

Owner, wholesale food business, male, 41

For years now, I've worn nothing but knee-length, black, woolen socks. I never have to worry about matching them up with each other or to my suit because black will match anything.

ME: What about in the summer?

Same thing, calf-length, black woolen socks.

ME: What about with a light suit?

Still black socks.

Public relations, male, mid-forties

Approximately 90% of my clothes are blue. All shades of blue. Right now I'm wearing a blue bathing suit, I have a blue dial on my watch and I have two lapus lazuli rings. As a matter of fact, one of the factors that influenced my enlisting in the Air Force is that they wear blue uniforms!

Salesman, advertising, male, 45

My socks and panties have to match. I have to be coordinated because you never know when you're going to whip off your pants and all that's left is socks and panties.

"Hairbender," female, 27
("I'd rather be known as a hairbender than a hairdresser because hairdressers remind me of wet sets and rollers and that whole beauty parlor trip which I don't feature. I bend your hair into what I want.").

When my wife gets up in the morning, before she throws her panties in the hamper, she dusts the furniture with them. When I ask her why she does it, she says, "Did I do that? . . . I didn't even notice."

Dental instrument mechanic, male, 64
His wife is a housewife, 56

I put my shirt and jacket on at the same time. It's quicker.

Bartender, male, 22

I have to have one brand new item of everything I might wear in my closet for a special occasion. I have a new pair of socks, a new pair of underwear, a new shirt, a new tie, a new pair of shoes and pajamas. I don't know exactly when I'm going to use them but when I do, I must replace them.

Manufacturer, blouses, male, 52

I always wear my watch on my right hand. The number of right-handed people who wear their watch on their right hand is about one in every ten million. It feels hideously uncomfortable on the left hand.

Musician, male, 37

I always fasten my bra in the front and then twist it around so the clip is in the back where it's supposed to be.

Teacher, female, 36

When my husband gets dressed in the morning, he puts on his pants, does up the zipper, buttons the button, buckles the belt, then goes and gets his shirt, unbuckles the belt, unbuttons the button, undoes the zipper, tucks in his shirt and then does it all up again.

Housewife, 30
Her husband is an airline pilot, 32

I never, ever wear my underpants right side out. I always wear them inside out to keep the little Bloomingdale's label from rubbing and chafing the small of my back.

Copywriter, male, 37

Before I put a shirt on, I hold it by the collar or neck and shake it out, even if it just arrived from the cleaners five minutes earlier. I just got into the habit of snapping out all of my shirts, including T-shirts.

Executive, male, 34

About ten or fifteen years ago, I noticed that a friend of mine, who has the same passion for shoes as I do, polished the soles of his shoes as well as the rest. He said it made them more waterproof and they lasted longer. That made perfectly good sense to me and I've been doing the same thing ever since. He was right.

Owner, foreign trade company, male, 40

I go nuts if all the hangers aren't facing in the same direction. The hooks must be pointed toward the back and all my clothes have to be facing one way. I think it's disorderly if they're not.

President, ad agency, male, 35

An old girl friend of mine wears white socks when she has sex. Nothing else, just white socks. It serves a dual purpose. It seems she must wear something when she has sex and also her toes get cold and the socks keep them warm.

Graduate Student, Male, 24
His ex-girlfriend is a graduate student, 23

The first article of clothing I put on in the morning is my hat. I always wear a wide-brimmed straw hat. If I have a shirt that has to go over my head, I don't remove the hat, I just pull it over the brim.

Shuttle bus driver, male, 58

I've always felt that I can run faster and feel much lighter with something white on my feet so I always wear white socks and sneakers when I participate in sports.

Orthodontist, male, 41

If I'm wearing a shirt and sweater with a T-shirt underneath, when I'm ready to get undressed, I'll unbutton the top button of my shirt, and pull the entire three layers off over my head at the same time.

Executive, male, 30

I have three pairs of lucky underwear. One's black, one's orange, and the third pair is yellow. Whenever I wear them, good things happen. And when I especially want something nice to happen, I'll wear one of them.

Beauty advisor, female, 24

My friend wears all her gold jewelry all the time because she's been ripped off three times in her apartment. She sleeps and does gymnastics wearing it. She has these massive rings on all her fingers, gobs of bracelets, at least twelve on each arm, and chains dripping down her front. I don't know how she manages to hold her body up. She never, ever takes them off.

Unemployed, female, 41
Her friend is a stewardess, 41

In order to put my socks on, I have to sit down and while I'm sitting it makes good sense to put my shoes on. Then I put my pants on. Otherwise, after I sit down to put my socks on I would have to stand up to put my pants on and then sit down again to put my shoes on.

ME: Why don't you put on your pants and then sit down and put your socks and shoes on?

Because I wear socks that come all the way up to my knees.

ME: You can roll up your pants.

That's too complicated.

Controller, male, 48

I iron only the front of my shirt and the sleeves because that's all that shows when I wear a suit. If I take the jacket off, I still have the vest on. It takes too much time to iron the whole shirt.

Systems analyst, male, 23

I have a closet full of size eight clothing although I'm a size fourteen. It bothers me to buy such a large size because I once was a size eight and I keep thinking that if I buy beautiful things in a small size it will be an incentive to lose weight. So far I haven't and I'm running out of things to wear even with a closet that's jam-packed.

Housewife, 53

When I buy a pair of shoes, I only try on one. I assume the other one will fit. No matter what, I keep them. I expect shoes to hurt.

Investment banker, male, 34

When I button my shirt, I start with the neck and I button alternate buttons down until I reach the bottom. Then I come up skipping buttons upwards. The result is that I always leave one button open and I could never figure out why. I've been doing it this way for years.

Marketing manager, male, 43

I only wear red socks. It makes my feet feel better. I like getting very dressed up in elegant clothing and having red socks. It's cheerful to look down and see them. I think Van Johnson always wore red socks. Otherwise, I'm a very conservative dresser.

Commercial photographer, male, 48

My mother has a batch of clothes for every season. As the seasons change, she brings down the new batch from the attic and wears them exactly in order. She does not select clothes according to her mood, she wears whatever is next in line so she doesn't have to think about her clothes.

Assistant buyer, female, 24
Her mother is a housewife, 55

I throw away clothes that I've worn when bad things have happened to me. I have no way of knowing whether I would be unlucky if I wore it again but I won't take the chance.

Lawyer, male, 32

I always check my fly before meeting people. You never know when things are going to be open at the wrong time.
ME: Doesn't it bother you that people see you checking?
Better that they see me checking than it being open!

Graphic designer, male, 28

There are two types of socks, Regular, which are worn during the day and Sleep-O's, which are worn to bed. When a regular sock is used up, I make a Sleep-O out of it by making the necessary alterations. You can't just go out and buy a pair of Sleep-O's. Sleep-O's are made not born. It's very important that they have enough give around the ankles so that it doesn't affect the circulation. They should also have a hole in the heel for air and be slightly damp at the toes to relax the calf muscles. By morning half the sock is off so the heel is exposed and only the toes are covered. I wear them as a protective covering because I can't stand the feeling of the sheets against my toes.

Executive, male, 44

I never take jewelry off unless it breaks off. I wash my hands and take a shower with my rings and necklaces.

Saleswoman, showroom, female, 25

I can't stand the thought of being seen in white underwear and black socks. I think it's almost as bad as wearing white socks with black shoes and pants. It just doesn't go. If I'm getting undressed, I make sure to take my socks off first or if I'm getting dressed, I do so in such an order that I can't be seen with just white underwear and black socks.

Student, male, 25

My father will put his arms through the T-shirt and read the label about four or five times, then he'll almost put the T-shirt over his head, bring it back down and read the label again. He's been doing this since I was a kid.

Sales rep, private telephone company,
female, 30

I select clothing that I'm going to wear from the right side of my closet and put fresh clothes on the left. It helps me decide what to wear.

Secretary, female, 44

I only wear dresses. I just don't feel comfortable in pants. I own one pair of jeans and that's only because someone gave them to me.

Student, female, 20

When I'm playing poker and I win, I will take the same socks, shirt and underwear I won in with me and change into them for the next game and each game after that until I lose. This is normal for a poker player.

Manufacturer, ladies' apparel, male, 44

When I was younger, I used to count red Volkswagens. Now I count Louis Vuitton bags. I don't think I've gone a day without seeing less than twenty-five.

Psychologist, female, 30

It gives me a feeling of freedom and comfort to wear as little as possible. That's why I never wear underwear or socks. About three years ago, my wife bought me a dozen pair of underwear. All the packages have remained unopened except one and I only wore that pair once or twice. I do succumb once in awhile and wear socks for an important occasion. People look at me a little funny in the winter when they look down and don't see socks. It bothers them more than it bothers me.

Salesman, carpet, male, 30

I never wear underwear or a T-shirt during the day but I do sleep in them just in case there's a fire. Or, if a robber breaks in, I don't want to have to go chasing after him balls-ass naked. Also sexually it's great to have underwear on.

Tattoo artist, male, 35

I change at least five times before I leave the house, even if it's just to walk the dog. I'm never happy with what I'm wearing.

Order processor, watch company, female, 25

I haven't worn underwear since World War II. I was in New Guinea and because it was very easy to get a fungus infection, the doctors there recommended that we try to keep our clothing as loose as possible. The air circulated better when we only wore our trousers and, as a result, I stopped wearing underwear entirely and haven't worn them since.

Stockbroker, male, 56

A friend of mine will not wear a pair of socks more than once. He has a drawerful of new socks and puts on a brand new pair every day. The kicker is that he throws them in the garbage after he wears them. I know this for a fact. I saw him do it. He doesn't like the feeling of socks that have already been worn or washed.

Salesman, fabric, male, 24
His friend is a salesman, apparel, male, 42

I still can't give up the sixties look. I'll probably be an aging hippie forever.

Social worker, female, 36

I don't think I've ever thrown a shoe away in my life. I have a great collection of old shoes. My wife eventually throws some away when she can't stand it anymore but I just can't bring myself to do it. Shoes are more comfortable as they get older.

Lawyer, male, 55

My parents' neighbor in suburbia wears a different outfit for every chore around the house. He has a Garage Attendant outfit for fixing the car. He has a Gardener outfit for landscaping. He has a Painter outfit for painting. He has a Chef outfit for cooking. He's very serious about this. I was up there visiting one time and I said to my father, "The guy next door must have hired a garage attendant to come fix his car." And my father said, "No, that's him."

Writer, female, 36
Her parents' neighbor is a dentist, 45

When my husband comes home from work, he changes his clothing, including his underwear. He has different color underwear for rainy and sunny days. He goes for light colors, whites, light blues and yellows on sunny days and darker colors, navies and grays, on rainy or overcast days.

Unemployed, female, 28
Her husband is a manufacturer, neckwear, 28

I wear my underpants over my pantyhose to hold them up.

Secretary, female, 35

I like to keep shoetrees in my sneakers because it gives them a much better look. The peculiar part is that I don't keep them in my other shoes.

Manufacturer, printing ink, male, late forties

Before I put clean socks in the drawer, I roll them up into a little ball and then flip them. When I unflip them, one is always inside out and it's too much of a bother to change it early in the morning so I always wear one sock inside out.

Scheduling coordinator, television, male, 25

No one can ever put anything away in my closet. My clothes are arranged in a particular order and if it's disrupted, I can't function or get dressed. My shirts are filed according to sleeve length— sleeveless to short to long. The clothes go from solids to plaids to stripes.

Real estate agent, female, 30

I'd rather go out and buy new underwear than do the laundry. There are about three drawers overflowing with underwear in my dresser.

Manufacturer, female, 33

For about fifteen years now, I have not exactly repeated an outfit. I may wear the same suit but with a different shirt and tie. I have an extensive wardrobe and I get a big kick out of this.

Manufacturer, luggage, male, 53

Whenever I throw shoes out, I insist on keeping the shoelaces. I have hundreds that I'll probably never use. I expect that someday, if a lace breaks on one of my shoes, I'll have an extra one to replace it, but generally, the lace breaks when I'm away from home so it doesn't do much good.

Salesman, male, 55

My boss has sixteen different-colored Lacoste sports shirts and he wears them in chromatic progression all through the summer. He starts with blue and goes right through the rainbow and then he starts over again. He wears each one twice but not two days in a row before washing it and that way he only has to do the laundry once for the summer. Sixteen shirts worn twice is good for six work-day weeks. His entire summer wardrobe is planned in advance.

Student, library science, female, 23
Her boss is a supervisor, library, male, 33

I never untie the laces in my shoes. I use a shoehorn to get the shoes on because I'm too lazy to bother with the laces.

Superintendent for general contractor, male, 27

When I was younger, I used to hang my pants on the wire hangers that came from the cleaners. It had that piece of paper across it that always used to come off. I swore that when I got older, I'd only use wooden hangers and I've kept that promise. When I bring clothes back from the cleaners, I throw the wire hangers out and replace them with wooden ones.

Controller, male, 31

The day that my great-great grandmother died, her daughter was wearing green. And the day that she died, my grandmother was wearing green. From that point on, my grandmother did not allow anyone in her family to wear green or buy anything green in her presence. If she saw anything green in the closet, she'd have a fit. So until she died, my mother, my father, my brother and I never bought anything green.

Student, female, 20

When I get undressed, I fold each article of clothing neatly before I throw them in the hamper.

Administrative assistant, commodity house,
male, 24

My boyfriend found a perfect solution to the Missing Sock Syndrome. The safety pin. He pins all his socks together so he never loses any. They don't come apart in the wash and all he has to do is reach into his drawer for a pair because they're already matched.

Teacher, special education, female, 27
Her boyfriend is a social worker, 27

I keep lists of the garments I wear during the week so I don't repeat them right away. If I notice on my list that I wore a particular outfit last Monday, I'll wait another week before I wear it again.

Fashion designer, female, 31

Whatever article of clothing I wear to a funeral or whatever article of clothing I'm wearing if have a bad experience, I will never wear again.

Housewife, female, 35

SCORE:

Clothing is just a big cover-up, anyway.

If you've uncovered one to seven quirks—You are below average and probably have a whole closet full of polyester leisure suits.

Eight to sixteen—You're getting there. I suggest you trade in some of your more conventional quirks for newer, more exciting ones.

Over seventeen—If I were you, I'd investigate the possibilities of a Peeping Tom on your premises.

The Howard Hughes syndrome

Believe it or not, there are more germs around than all the roaches in New York City. And they're even harder to get rid of. Not even boric acid will do the trick.

Germs congregate most frequently in the following places:

1. Other People's Mouths

   To protect ourselves from possible contamination if someone should ask for a sip of our drink, here's what can be done:

   A. Turn glass around before handing over and carefully observe exact position Other Mouth has made contact and avoid that spot.

   B. Say, "I'll save you some."

   C. Say, "Why don't you finish it, I'm really not thirsty." Item C has extra bonus of being thought of as Nice Guy.

   D. Smile when drink is returned and pour into nearest plant when Other Person is not looking.

   E. Say, "I'll buy you one." Item E is least desirable because of the expense.

   Exception 1: When we kiss Other People.

   When we kiss Other People, the germs move over.

   Exception 2: Eating from Other People's Plates.

   Other People's Plates are relatively germ-free. Especially if it has Häagen-Dazs coffee ice cream on it.

2. *Other People's Toothbrushes*
   No matter how much you wash or shake another person's toothbrush, the germs do not fall off. They cling. So we must never use Other People's Toothbrushes. Not even toothbrushes of Other People we kiss. If we keep our toothbrush in the same holder as Other People, however, the germs cannot jump onto our toothbrush. Even if their toothbrush is in the adjacent hole. But only if the bristles do not touch.
3. *Other People's Behinds*
   Other People's Behinds are full of very bad germs. So we must never sit directly on Other People's Toilets. We can either cover the germs with paper and hope that they do not crawl above it. Or we can squat. And hope that they do not like what they see a whole lot.
4. *Other People's Money*
   But these are not very harmful germs. We can easily live with them.

The few areas from which germs are repelled:
1. *Bloomingdale's*
   Everything in Bloomingdale's is guaranteed germ-free. In fact, they are highly recommended for your health.
2. *Warren Beatty*
3. *Certain Foods*
   You can apply the following principle to determine which foods do not have a lot of germs: the more the calories, the fewer the germs. A flaming chocolate crêpe has virtually no germs.
And with that, I wash my hands of this.

The last time I went into a public bathroom was in 1959. I was six years old and I really had to go. I don't believe doctors who say you can't contract a social disease by sitting on a dirty toilet.

Salesman, male, 26

When I buy fruits or vegetables, I completely wash them with soap and water to disinfect them before I put them in the refrigerator. It has to do with the fact that they're so filthy by the time they get to us. Birds do their thing while they're still on the tree. All kinds of people handle them. I won't eat fruits or vegetables anywhere unless I know for sure they were washed with soap.

Engineer, male, 30

I always hold a coffee cup that has a handle in my left hand even though I'm right-handed. My reasoning is that there are fewer left-handed people in the world, therefore fewer people drink on that side so in my mind, I think there are less germs on that side.

Graphic designer, female, 30

I drink where the handle of the cup is because no one drinks there.

Musician, female, 28

When I go to a restaurant, I hold a coffee cup with the handle right opposite my face so my mouth touches the part of the rim directly opposite the handle. There's less chance of contracting any kind of disease.

Hairdresser, male, 29

I try never to touch food directly with my hands even if they're clean. If there is a napkin available, I'll wrap it around the sandwich or whatever it is I'm eating. If not, I'll eat all around the spot I'm holding and throw that piece away.

Architect, male, 37

When you'd buy an ice cream cone a few years ago, the guy behind the counter would reach for the cone with a napkin and then put the scoop in. Lately, he reaches for the cone, puts the scoop inside and then hands you a napkin and it drives me up a wall. I don't want him to touch my ice cream cone.

Speech pathologist, female, 26

I insist that my secretary clean the receiver of my telephone with disinfectant every morning. I must start the day with a clean phone.

Professional investor, male, 37

When I get into a taxi, I never let any bare part of my body touch the seat. I sit forward so my head doesn't touch. And I wear gloves all year so my hands don't contact anything directly that masses of people have used.

Saleswoman, 29

I hate to walk past a bum on the street because I always think that if the wind blows in my direction, his germs will get all over me. So I stay as far away as possible as I hurry by.

Stewardess, 31

When my father goes on vacation he takes his own silverware and salt and pepper with him. My mother is embarrassed, she thinks he's a nut.

Teacher, female, 25
Her father is retired, 73

When making a salad or preparing a drink, if a piece of lettuce or an ice cube falls into the sink, it's immediately thrown away, regardless of how clean the sink may be. It's my crazy thing about germs. If someone else is making a drink and I know the ice cube fell into the sink but was used anyway, I will drink it but it will bother me tremendously.

College professor, male, 38

In a restaurant, before I drink out of a cup or glass, I pour some water or coffee on my napkin and wipe all around the rim.

Housewife, 59

My mother sprays my father all over his body with Lestoil before he gets into bed. He doesn't take a shower every day and she thinks he may have germs. She disinfects the poor man.

Waitress, 40
Her mother is a housewife, 59

I can't stand it if anyone, including my husband, touches my pillow. I must be the only one to touch it.

Saleswoman, 28

I have a habit of cleaning off the silverware before I use it, whether it's clean or dirty.

ME: Is that only in a restaurant?

No, I do it at home also.

ME: What about if you're visiting someone?

I usually manage to do it although I try not to make it too obvious.

Writer/producer, male, 26

When I enter an elevator, I take a deep breath and hold it during the entire ride. I pray that I don't meet anyone I know so I won't be forced to exhale and start a conversation and inhale everyone's germs.

Manufacturer, jewelry, male, 35

No matter how heavy a shopping bag is that I'm carrying, I will never put it down on the floor. It would get disgusting germs all over it.

Housewife, 59

I buy only white toilet paper because I know someday they'll discover that the dyes in the colored ones are bad for you.

Housewife, female, 61

I always discard the first couple of squares of toilet paper in a public john because the previous person probably touched it.

Bookkeeper, female, 47

Before I use any of my dishes, I rinse them off although I may have just taken them out of the dishwasher that very morning. It's a habit I inherited from my mother who feels that they could collect dust in the cabinet.

Housewife, female, 25

In public bathrooms, I won't touch the doorknob after I've washed my hands. I use a paper towel to open the door and hold the door with my foot while I throw the paper towel in the receptacle.

Diamond dealer, male, 55

When I take a young lady out for the first time, I take a penicillin pill the next day.

Harness driver, male, 35

Every time I touch money, no matter how often, I wash my hands. When I hand my husband money for tolls while driving, I wipe my hands on a wet rag which I always keep in the car for that purpose. If I find money on the sidewalk, I use a tissue to pick it up and wrap it with, and when I get home, I wash the coin or bill with soap and water.

Assistant upholsterer, female, 59

An out-of-town friend of mine came to visit for a few weeks and I noticed when I went into the bathroom that his toothbrush was sticking up in the holder. So I pushed it down. The next time I went into the bathroom, it was pushed back up so I pushed it down again. This went on for awhile until I finally asked him about it. He explained that the idea of the bristles actually touching the holder which is full of bacteria really turned him off. That's why he twists his toothbrush so it doesn't slide all the way down.

Account executive, female, 29
Her friend is a draftsman, 31

My quirk is that I will not let anybody drink from my glass or eat from my plate. NOBODY. EVER. Not even my family, my boyfriend or my friends. Someone just asked me for a sip and I told them that when I was finished, I'd leave something over.

Nurse, female, 33

I always felt that if I touched the area between my toes, I would never be able to wash my hands clean enough. I'd always have germs on them. To avoid contacting there directly, I use a cloth or a Q-tip or just spread my toes, drip the soap in and let the water run over my feet.

Diamond dealer, male, 55

I always break Q-tips before I use them. Somehow, I always think that germs would travel from one end to the other so by breaking them, they can't get across.

Lawyer, male, 31

I keep my toothbrush in a traveling case at all times so it doesn't get dusty or dirty. Each time I use the toothbrush, it goes back in its case.

Jewelry waxer, female, 50

My problem is that I cannot drive a car unless it's immaculately clean. If the car is dirty, I feel the same way.

Doorman, male, 31

Before I open a can, I wash the top off with soap and water so any dirt or germs don't get inside as I'm opening it. That's what my mother told me.

Banker, male, 26

My boyfriend will take out a piece of note paper or tissue to hold onto the subway pole. He doesn't like to touch it directly.

Actress/dancer, 31
Her boyfriend is a manager, TV production
company, 46

I towel-dry my hair and if the towel falls on the floor, I have to use a new towel for fear that germs and bacteria are on the floor.

Typographer, male, 29

There's no way I'll go into a swimming pool because people urinate in the water and go in with different skin diseases and God knows what else. I will go into the ocean because it's so vast and because the wastes don't seem to bother the fish.

Tailor, male, 47

I would never flush a public toilet with my hand. I use my foot or my elbow or find some other way of doing it.

Manager, pharmaceutical company, male, 32

SCORE:

Use this table to determine whether you are suffering from a mild or severe case of The Howard Hughes Syndrome:

Less than five similar—You're the type who would ask for a sip of my Coke.

Five to ten—You're the type who would ask for a sip of my Coke but would wipe the bottle neck first.

Over ten—You would rather die than ask for a sip of my Coke. In fact, you would order tea because it's been boiled. But you would ask for a paper cup and wipe the spoon. (By the way, there's really no need to be reading with those gloves on. And take that surgical mask off, for God's sake.)

Now I've heard everything!

Ever notice how you stop and give a perfectly smooth, flat sidewalk your nastiest, most accusing how-dare-you look after you've tripped over your own two feet?

Did you start reading the last page of this book first?

Are you twirling your hair? Ah, hah! I caught you in action.

How many times do you check the knobs on your stove to make sure they're off before you leave the house?

Do you refuse to buy the top newspaper even though it's in perfect condition?

Does your husband manage to get a spot of grease on a fresh shirt or a new tie five minutes after he puts it on? And he doesn't have to be eating.

If you are not a mailman and you stand outside in the rain or snow for hours, then you must be a New Yorker waiting to see a movie. Now tell me that's not a quirk?

Are you biting your fingernails? Toenails? Maybe you're picking at your feet, or God forbid, worse? And reading my book, yet.

Does your pinkie extend when you're drinking out of a glass? Can you continue drinking when you try to bring it in next to the other fingers?

Do you wait for the telephone to ring at least twice before you answer even if you're right on top of it?

If there's no one else in a bathroom, do you walk out without washing your hands?

Are you twirling your hair again?

Sound familiar? You're thinking maybe you should see your shrink three times a week instead of two? Forget it. If you do most or even all of these things, you've got plenty of company. These are some of the more common unconscious little rituals and habits we all share.

Some idiosyncrasies you might be somewhat embarrassed about, others you claim sole ownership to because of their ingenious complexity. People will either think of you fondly because of them or it will irk the hell out of them and they won't want anything to do with you. Let's face it, they're what make you, you.

The trick to appearing normal is to hang out with people who are quirkier than you. But the bottom line is, nobody's playing with a full deck.

———

From the time I was about three, there was an old cliché that if you stepped on a crack, you'd break your mother's back. So, to this day, I still tend to avoid the cracks in the sidewalk as I'm walking along.

Physician, male, 50

My work involves house calls, ten to twelve a day, and I'm in and out of the car. Every time I get in and turn the key, I light up a cigarette. I have to have it as soon as the car starts. It's part of driving.

Electrician, male, 36

One Sunday when I was in the army, all my friends were away on a weekend pass and I was stuck with guard duty. I was walking up and down a lonely road with my rifle singing, "My Melancholy Baby." Ever since then, when I go buy my newspaper every Sunday, I quietly sing "My Melancholy Baby" on the way there.

Carpenter, male, 59

Every time I go on an airplane, I thoroughly clean my apartment, especially the bathroom, and make sure it's immaculate in case I don't come back. I don't want anyone to come into a dirty apartment and say, 'This is how that guy lived!'

Manufacturer, paper cones, male, 32

I cannot sit in a restaurant or any public place with my back to the major entrance. I like to see who's coming in.

Writer, male, 29

As soon as I sit down at my desk, I open the top middle desk drawer. I leave it open the entire time I sit there. For some reason I feel terribly uncomfortable if it's closed.

Security guard, female, 19

Playing tennis, if I fault on the first serve, I won't use the same ball again for the second serve.

Administrative supervisor, pharmacy, female, 23

When I go home to my apartment, although I know there's nobody there because I live alone, I always yell, 'Hello, I'm home!'

Sound engineer, male, 31

I love to watch Spanish television and movies for hours at a time and I don't understand a word of Spanish. They have great vampire movies. It keeps me entertained.

Manufacturer, ladies' sportswear, male, 30

I call the weather every day during the summer. On weekends, after I call New York weather, I call Long Island weather. I want to make sure that Fire Island and the Hamptons don't have better weather than we do.

Media buyer, female, "thirtyish"

I prefer lighting my cigarettes with boxed matches. I never throw away the used matches. I put them back in the box and continue to do this until the box is filled with used matches. Then I discard the whole box. It's hard to tell the good matches from the used ones at night but I just keep striking until one works. I developed this habit in the Israeli army because we weren't permitted to litter. It just stayed with me.

Electronics technician, male, 25

Whenever I read a magazine or newspaper, I start at the back and work my way to the front.

Carpenter, male, 40

I always stir or shake something thirteen times and I tap off the excess fluid from the utensil thirteen times. Even if what I'm stirring is thoroughly mixed in three or four stirs, I still continue stirring to thirteen. If it needs more than thirteen stirs, I then go to thirty-nine. It's for superstitious reasons.

Would not give profession, male, 58

I play William Tell's Overture on my knuckles. If you give me a beat I could play anything because they go endlessly.

Student, female, 17
(She's terrific!)

I never tell my age. My ex-wife or her lawyer don't even know my age.

Business executive, male

It just kills me to put the first piece of garbage in a clean garbage bag. In fact, many times I find myself running to the incinerator with one wrapper, or can or banana peel so I don't have to dirty the clean bag.

Masseuse, 58

After I use one of those wash 'n dry wet naps, I fold it up again and put it back in the envelope. I tend to border on the obsessive compulsive in terms of things being in their place and this is just part of it.

College administrator, female, 29

My chintzy friend will drive around for forty-five minutes looking for a parking space but he never finds one and has to put his car in a lot anyway. Meanwhile he keeps his friends waiting, he wastes all that gas looking plus the cost of the garage. That's why it's taking him so long to get here.

Marketing representative, male, 25
His friend is a lawyer, 25

I have to break a date with a guy three times before I finally agree to go out with him. I like the persistent ones.

ME: Do most call back?

A lot of them don't. Just the ones that find me worth waiting for.

Manufacturer, jewelry, female, 33

When entering almost any indoor place I empty my pockets and put the contents in one little pile. It generally contains my eyeglasses, pen, key, wrist watch and money. I believe it's a way of expressing my territoriality. It becomes my little spot and if anybody else puts something on my little spot, it bothers me and I will move my things or theirs. In a restaurant, my little spot is one corner of the table. I've never lost anything because all I have to do is take everything off that spot and put it back in my pocket when I'm ready to leave.

College professor, male, 38

My father thinks it's New Years every Fourth of July. We have a big Fourth of July party every year and he keeps checking his watch. When it's twelve o'clock, he says, "Happy New Year!"

Waitress, 40
Her father is a cab driver, 67

I can't ride backwards in any moving vehicle. I have to be facing in the same direction the bus or train is traveling.

Interior designer, female, 57

I never look at the paper without having done the crossword puzzle first, no matter what the headlines are. The world could be ending but it will have to wait until I finish the puzzle.

Unemployed, female, 31

At the age of thirty, I still read comic books. I have a subscription to ten of them . . . Batman, Superman, Aquaman, all of them. During the week, the pressures of the job are too much so who wants to read about the devaluation of the dollar. I'd rather read about Batman catching criminals.

Manufacturer, ladies' sportswear, male, 30

I enjoy smoking cigarettes stuck between the prongs of a fork or at the end of a straw.
Me: Does it work at the end of a straw?
It works very well at the end of a straw.
Me: Why do you do this?
To break up the monotony of the day. I'm not even conscious of when I do it.

Administrative assistant, male, 25

I have to be completely naked when I'm cleaning.

Theatre director, female, 29

When what I'm doing, whether it's watching TV or listening to a teacher lecture, isn't absorbing my full attention, I suddenly become aware that I've been pulling my split ends apart. It can be very embarrassing when I realize I've been doing it in public. People probably think I have cooties.

Student, female, 22

I always have a song in my head and I walk to the beat of it.

Exterminator, male, 27

I like to appear neat and organized. I have a wonderful system for achieving this . . . I throw everything in the closet. Laundry, magazines, all sorts of junk, just as long as I can close the door.

Dietician, female, 35

When I pick up my mail, if it looks like one piece is interesting, say, a love note, or a check from somebody who's past due, I save that letter for last. When I have time to savor it, then I open it.

Textile wholesaler, male, 33

In all of my long, very straight, fine hair, I have one very coarse, frizzy, curly hair. I periodically search for that hair and pull it out.

Graphic designer, female, 27

I'm a neat freak. When a perforated form has been torn off, I'll tear off every little piece that's been left on. Also, if something is stapled in a manner that is not nice and neat, I will take the staple out, adjust the papers so they're positioned exactly in line, and then re-staple it.

Office manager, television network, female, 39

If I turn around to say hello to somebody, I have to turn around the other way to unwind. Or, if the telephone cord twirls around my leg or body, rather than just step out of it, I have to untwirl the other way.

Graduate student, female, 22

When my husband kisses me on my right cheek, I ask him to kiss me on my left cheek, or vice versa, to balance them out.

Production manager for printing broker, female, 25

If I close one eye, I have to close the other eye to make sure they both open and close the same amount of times.

Film editor, male, 32

When I write, I have to have a cigarette in my other hand for balance.

Management consultant, male, 37

I have to feel symmetrical at all times. If I put a bobby pin on one side of my head, there has to be another one in the same place on the other side. If I scratch one arm, I scratch the same spot on the other arm. Otherwise I feel unequal.

Registered nurse, female, 34

I twirl my hair because I'm nervous and it feels good!

Insurance adjustor, female, 31

My neighbors think I'm crazy. I don't cut the lawn in the normal, up and down way. I cut it in spiral fashion, working from the outside around toward the center. I love the way the tracks look when it's cut.

Chauffeur, male, 25

If I'm given a sheet of ruled paper to write on, I automatically write either perpendicular or diagonal to the rules because I don't need somebody else to organize me. I can organize myself.

Sailor, male, 43

Although I don't use it, to be able to read anything, even a personal letter, I must hold a pen or a pencil in my hand. It probably stems from my school days when I used to underline in the text books and now I find the habit has stayed with me.

Assistant treasurer, bank, female,
would not give age

On any screw-on cap, I'll screw it on three times and that's the end of it. If it isn't completely screwed on, it doesn't matter.

Nurse, female, 28

I have this crazy habit. I can't help myself. About 15 times a day, I automatically come out with bird calls. It's become a habit. Sometimes I talk to myself in bird language.

Elevator starter, male, 27
(He's really good!)

When I go to a movie with my date, I buy two tickets but I manage to hand them only one as we're walking in, so I have an extra one. When we come out, I look for someone interesting waiting in line to buy a ticket and I hand them my extra one. I just say, "Here, enjoy the movie." People are interesting. When I give them the ticket, they never say anything, they're so stunned. They just look at the ticket in amazement as I walk away. I've done it over a hundred times during the last ten years and it works about 75% to 80% of the time. When I'm caught, I always have the extra ticket. It's my way of feeling a little like Robin Hood, stealing from the rich and giving to the poor.

Salesman, male, 29

My toes curl in when I'm excited about something. Sometimes both feet at the same time but generally alternating. When I see Ella Fitzgerald my toes curl.

Governess, female, 19

I never smile. I don't want to put any wrinkles in my face.

ME: What if you hear a good joke?

I never smile.

ME: Do you have all your teeth?

Yes.

Taxi driver, male, 37
(This was confirmed by his friends and nothing I
could say would make him smile!)

I won't write with red or black ink. Any other color is fine. If someone hands me a pen that has red or black ink, I'll ask if they have another one. Those of my friends who are aware of my quirk automatically hand me an alternate color. I like red and black in just about anything else.

Secretary, female, 31

I won't use anything but a black felt tip pen in business. It's probably a luck factor.

Restaurateur, male, 36

I count things. I count the squares in a chain link fence. I count the windows in a building, the tiles in a wall, anything with definite divisions running in a pattern. I haven't the foggiest idea why.

Attorney, male, 35

When I use a paper towel in the kitchen, if I haven't used it completely, I'll fold it, put it in my pocket and use it again later to dust the furniture or wipe my hands.

Engineer, male, 30

My aunt will wash, set and dry her hair at home before going to the hairdresser. She likes to look her best at all times, including on her way to get her hair done.

Housewife, 29
Her aunt is a seamstress, 49

I smoke cigarettes backwards with the lighted part in my mouth because it feels good. It's impossible to burn yourself if you know the proper method which I've mastered over a period of many years.

Pianist, male, 25

I can't start working until I get all my pencils sharpened and lined up. It just feels neat and orderly and kind of organizes my thoughts.

Lawyer, male, 31

I keep my watch five minutes fast at all times and I go by that time, so I'm never late for an appointment.

Numerologist, male, 35

My reverse quirk is that I make an effort to break any habit or any consistent thing that I might be doing. If I find I've done something a certain way six times in a row and it can be done another way, I will deliberately do it another way.

C.P.A., male, 46

I like the resonant sound when I pat my stomach. I play it to the rhythm of music that's playing or some tune that's going through my head. I'll deny this if you ever mention it to my patients.

Physician, male, 36
(He did a great demonstration!)

When I'm tired or upset or depressed, I get a towel, fold it, put it in my mouth, and scream like a maniac. Then I feel better!

Hairdresser, male, 25

If I visit someone in their home and there's more than one entrance, I must leave through the same door I came in. Under no circumstances will I leave by a different doorway. If I go in the front door, I go out the front door. If I go in the back, I go out the back.

Manager of consumer affairs, corporation,
female, 37

In my younger days I used to play basketball. I'd often measure the steps from one part of the basketball court to the other so I would know automatically how many steps I could take in a dribble. This habit has remained with me because I find myself counting the steps from one place to another such as from the bus stop to my home or from my parking spot to my home. From the bus stop to my home there are 240 steps, walking at a leisurely pace. From my garage to where I exit from my home, there are 360 steps. Why I do this, I don't know. It has no practical value although I can't see any loss in doing it!

Physician, male, 64

I let the fingernails on my pinkies grow until they fall off naturally or break off. It's an idiosyncrasy I developed some years ago. I don't know why. They make great letter openers, although I don't grow them specifically for that purpose.

Mover, male, fifties

Before I take something from someone—food, an object, anything, I smell it first. I put my head forward and sniff before I touch.

Stockbroker, female, 34

If I'm in my car and I realize I've forgotten something, I can't just back the car up, even if there isn't any traffic and I'm only a few feet from my house. I have to go all the way around the block to come back. If I go over the same path, I feel like I'm not progressing.

Presser, dry cleaning store, male, 30

If there's a specific article in the fourth section of the newspaper that I want to read, I can't just open the paper to that article. I must start with page one and read from the beginning in order up to that column.

Actor, 42

I keep a band-aid on my tennis racket, near the handle and I always play with the band-aid face up. I've never replaced it . . . it's the same old crusty band-aid I put on the racket when I first got it. Don't ask me why.

Owner, construction company, male, 36

I've been saving all my fingernails and toenails in an old mayonnaise jar since I was in the ninth grade. I put a little Brut in there so it smells good, although protein doesn't decay. I just got into the habit and it's hard to break.

HIS ATTRACTIVE WIFE: It's true. Sometimes he shows it to people who come over as a joke.

Sales Manager, jewelry company, male, 29

My girlfriend puts on her make-up, mascara and all, the night before to save time in the morning.

Secretary, female, 22
Her girlfriend is a student, 22

After smoking a joint, I always eat the roach. It tastes nice.

College professor, male, 38

I like to walk around the apartment naked and I love young men. That's why I'm with one.

Unemployed, female, 63

When I want to remember something in the morning, I take a paper napkin, poke a hole through it and hang it on the door-knob. When I leave my apartment, the napkin reminds me that there was something I wanted to remember, like taking oranges with me to the office or stopping at the shoemaker to have my boots fixed and so on. It happened only once that upon seeing the napkin, I couldn't remember what I had to do.

Bookkeeper, female, 46

I fake a sneeze when I fart so people won't hear me.

Student, female, 17

When I watch a ball game, if the team I'm rooting for is doing well, I will stay in whatever position I'm sitting in for the rest of the game. I wouldn't budge or get up for anything. If they do well the way I'm sitting, then I'll just stay that way.

Mailman, 55

When I want the Yankees or the Knicks to win, I wear special good luck clothes and sit in a certain position on the floor in front of the television set. I also do it for the Giants but it hasn't been working too well for them the last few years.

Senior vice president, ad agency, male, 44

My husband's idiosyncrasy is his inability to throw anything out. For example, we have a collection of about twenty coffee cans on top of our refrigerator because we may need one someday. And then there's the idiosyncrasy of my friend who must arrange them neatly every time she comes over.

Medical student, female, 24
Her husband is a medical student, 25
Her friend is a medical student, 25

Rather than lug the vacuum cleaner around, chasing the dirt, I bring the dirt to the vacuum cleaner. I keep the vacuum cleaner inside a closet and just sweep the dirt there. All I have to do is reach in, push the button and suction up the dirt.

Salesman, paper, 50

My friend's mother collects empty margarine tubs and lids for re-use. She uses only a few but she has more than a few around the house. They're all over. There are dozens and dozens stacked on shelves, in drawers, everywhere.

Student, male, 21
His friend's mother is a teacher, 46

Every once in a while I put my finger in my belly button and smell my finger.

ME: Does it smell good?

Not really. Some people pick their nose, I do this.

Buyer, womens' apparel, male, 55

I turn on the TV as soon as I walk into my apartment regardless of what's on. It's a surrogate person.

National ad manager, corporation, male, 30

Whenever I have an empty container, it could be an empty tube of toothpaste or a jar, I always put the cap back on before I discard it.

Investment analyst, male, 36

When my mother includes some good news or a happy thought in a letter to anyone, she'll put a little smiling face after the sentence. If she has a bit of bad news or a sad comment, for example, "the old dog died," she'll put a little frowning face after the sentence.

Sea captain, male, 41
His mother is a housewife, 61

As an act of civic pride and duty, I always stop at every Don't Walk sign and wait until the green Walk sign flashes. And, in fact, I admonish people who go against it as a sign of civil disobedience and irresponsibility. The city spends a great amount of money on the installation and maintenance of these devices, literally millions of dollars. The electricity is used twenty-four hours a day, 365 days a year. They have laws against jay walking because of the hundreds of pedestrian deaths. But if you follow the law, people look at you like you're strange.

Attorney, male, 38

My ex-boss has a device above his desk that looks somewhat like a clock. It has the numbers one through ten and the word "Bell Ringer" on it in a circle and a moveable cardboard hand. He uses it as a rating system for the work that is presented to him. It used to drive us crazy. He'd sit there for half an hour and not say a word about the work after the person did three hours of singing and dancing and carrying on and then he would get up and move the dial to one of the numbers or all the way to Bell Ringer depending on how little or how much he liked the idea.

Copywriter, female, 36
Her ex-boss is a vice president, ad agency, 50

I talk to myself all the time. I have complete conversations and giggle and answer my own questions. It drives a lot of people crazy.

Art director, female, 27

If my wife forgets something in the house and goes back for it, she'll sit on a chair and count to ten before she leaves again.

Manager, delicatessen, male, 65
His wife is an IBM operator, 58

I never go back for something if I forget it. It's bad luck. I'll have somebody else go back but I won't go back for it myself.

Saleswoman, showroom, 25

I keep skis on the roof of my car all year round so I can find my car in a parking lot. Other people may leave the rack on the roof in the winter but no one actually keeps the skis there because they're afraid of being ripped off. Mine are old and in very bad condition so no one's ever taken them. The big disadvantage to this is that my car is well known to my friends and I can't go to an automatic car wash so my car is always dirty.

Physician, male, 28

Before I begin reading a book, it's very important that I look at the ending to find out what happened.

Teacher, female, 36

If I should hear fire engines near my building or smell smoke or see it in the hall, I immediately grab my two favorite puppets, my portfolio, and my American Indian turquoise necklaces and fly out the door. I wait in the lobby until I'm absolutely sure everything is all right.

Marionette maker, female, 27

When I'm three or four blocks from my office, many times, I'll suddenly think, "Did I lock the door?" Although I know I did, there's a compulsion to get off the bus and go back to check. This has happened several times and I always feel very silly because the door has always been locked.

Store manager, male, 56

I must step off the curb with my right foot even if I have to shift my feet.

Banker, male, 42

My mother was a meticulously clean woman. She was very proud of the way she kept her house. She would iron all the rags and fold them neatly before she put them in the rag drawer.

Book designer, female, 45
Her mother was a housewife.

I'm constantly checking the door to my apartment, the gas stove, the car doors, my stereo and all on-off, open-close switches to make sure they're off. I've almost broken the knob on my stereo. Sometimes I go all the way back upstairs to make sure I locked the door, knowing inside that I really did. It's gotten to be an obsession.

Traffic coordinator, ad agency, male, 22

Whenever I pass a cemetery or funeral home, I must say to myself, "May all the dead rest in peace."

Housewife, 59

My husband sits sideways to the television set and then turns his head to watch. It's the strangest thing.

Teacher, female, 33
Her husband is a professor, biology, 37

I straighten up for the maid so it won't be too messy.

Sales representative, manufacturer, male, 30

One of the small satisfactions in my life is drawing a red line through something on a list of things I'm supposed to do. It's one thing finished in a frustrating, unfinished world. I'll even add something I've accomplished to the list which was not originally on it. Then I have the gratification of crossing it off.

Homicide detective, female, 46

I pray for my dog every night and he's been dead for five years.

Account executive, male, 27

Normal couples have arguments over the toothpaste tube, we have constant hassles about the car armrest. She likes it up for her pocketbook, I like it down for my arm. When I do the driving, I insist on having it down and shove her pocketbook over to her side.

Physician, male, 28

My wife invites me to go out with her girlfriends when she has to go out of town. That way she knows who I'm with. In fact, I'm with my wife's girlfriend right now.

Theatrical designer, male, 30

If I don't get through the Sunday Times, I'll save the magazine section and the book review section. Right now, there's a stack about twelve inches high at home. When I have a day off, I take the oldest one to the park to read. I'd feel guilty taking a more current one.

Salesman, male, 55

After I've been out somewhere, I look in the mirror when I come back in the house to see how I looked to other people.

Nurse, female, 39

Whenever I have a newspaper in front of me or a blank sheet of paper, instead of doodling, I write down department store names. I always start off with Bloomingdale's, then continue with Alexander's, Macy's, May's, and Gimbels' and end up listing a whole slew of department stores. Sometimes I'll just keep writing Bloomingdale's in different ways and styles. I guess the reason I do it is because I worked there for six years and I used to have pens imprinted with Bloomingdale's which I would see and unconsciously start to write.

Assistant supervisor, insurance company,
female, 24

The music is always on in the car and I sing along with it. When I get to an unknown area, the sound affects my vision and I must have complete silence to be able to concentrate on the direction.

Branch coordinator, manufacturer, female, 29

After I mail a letter, I have to open the lid again to make sure the letter went down the slot. It hasn't gotten stuck yet but I still have to check.

Assistant product manager, female, 23

My husband would rather drive miles out of his way than ask for directions. He says he's not willing to take somebody else's directions, he likes to be in control. He's right. He has excellent control over how to waste time and gasoline and where to find the most uninteresting places. I've been on the road more than a traveling salesman. It's gotten so that when I sit down, I expect trees to pass by.

Housewife, 45
Her husband is an executive, 52

If we're in a store and we're not sure where something is, my boyfriend will absolutely refuse to ask sales clerks, even if they're standing right in front of him.

Assistant magazine editor, female, 23
Her boyfriend is a theatre consultant, 25

A friend of mine grows a beard and shaves it off once a year. He saves the hair and keeps it in plastic bags which he dates. Some people save string—he saves hair.

Product manager, male, 28
His friend is a court officer, 32

I'm a Pack-passer—I can't stay behind a pack of cars. I have to be out in front and I weave in and out until I get there. I can go 50 m.p.h. once I'm in front of the pack unless a car passes me, then I have to pass them back.

Social worker, male, 37

Before I throw an empty can out, I rinse it and get all the gook out. I have immaculate garbage.

Media planner, ad agency, male, 21

When I'm walking down the street with a date, I'll have my date walk near the curb and I will walk close to the buildings in case a car skids. It will hit him first.

Teacher, physical education, female, 23

I can't stand waiting at a red light, so I always walk in whichever direction the traffic light is green as I go toward my destination.

Owner, boutique, female, 32

In my family, when we send a letter to someone we're fond of, we turn the stamp upside down to signify an extra, added, I love you. We extend this to our boyfriends and girlfriends. My mother has written me a couple of letters without the stamp upside down and I've called her immediately afterwards asking if she hated me.

Student, female, 20

When I sit for a long time, quite often I find that my hip joints go out of place. In the middle of anywhere, it could be Grand Central Station, if I have a bad hip problem, I'll throw my leg back in an arabesque so I can pop my hip back into place.

Actress, 41

My husband never throws out used tissues. He folds them up and puts them in his pocket. It's very annoying when the shirt goes through the wash and the tissue shreds and gets all over the rest of the clothes.

Physician, female, 29
Her husband is a physician, 29

The first thing I read in a newspaper is the obituary column to make sure my name isn't there.

Speech pathologist, male, 54

If I'm walking down the left side of the street but my destination is on the right side, I will cross over, as soon as possible, to the side of the street where my destination is.

ME: Why?

I don't know, I just have a very strong feeling that I'd like to be on the side of the street where I'm going.

Professor, art, female, 28

I love to move my apartment furniture around. I like change for the sake of change. Not only does the placement of the furniture change, the use of the room changes as well. The living room can become the bedroom, the bedroom can become another room, my son's room can become my room. Sometimes I like sleeping in a large room and sometimes I like sleeping in a small room. I had a couch in the kitchen for awhile which was great. When my son comes home from a holiday, he never knows where his room will be or which room is being used for what because it's always different. It's become a family joke.

Dancer, female, 38

When I read something, or see something or think about something, I will mentally type out the thought on my toes. My little toes control the shift keys and I use my big toes for the space bar. I'm real fast at it too.

Model, female, 24

I'm very nearsighted. Not only do I see better with my eyeglasses, I also hear better with them. I think it's because we all unconsciously lip read to some extent and without my glasses, of course, I can't see the lip movements as well. But my quirk is that if the telephone rings, and I don't have my glasses on, I must run and quickly find them before I answer because otherwise I won't hear as well over the phone! That doesn't make any sense because, naturally, you can't lip read over the phone.

Graphic designer, female, 28

The Oriental people carry a stick that's about three or four inches long and is shaped like a miniature spoon at one end. It can be made of ivory, bamboo, silver, or gold, depending on how wealthy the owner is. They use it to clean their ears. Rather than carry one around with me, I decided to grow my pinkie nails long and use them for that purpose.

Owner, chinese restaurant, male, 48

I still suck my thumb. It nurtures me if I'm sick or hurt or tired and I just want to go to sleep and cuddle up.

Hairdresser, male, 33

I cannot deal cards unless the pinkie of my dealing hand is extended as though I were holding a cup. If somebody says to me, "Why is your pinkie out?" and I try to bring it in, I can't deal the cards!

Furrier, male, 33

I clean the rooms in the house in alphabetical order. I start with the bathroom, then I do the bedroom, then the kitchen and then the living room. That always seemed to me to be the best way to clean the house.

Graduate student, female, 24

I love fishing but I hate to bait my own hook or pull the fish off the hook. It smells up my fingers so I have my friend do it for me. If my friend isn't available, I don't go fishing.

Salesman, clothing, male, 29

I get a real charge out of sticking my tongue up my girlfriend's nose. She thinks it's the most disgusting thing in the world and I have to prove to her that it's not.

Psychiatric counselor, male, 27

One side of our couch is mine and the other side is my husband's. When we have company and a guest sits on his side, my husband won't object, he'll just give the person a nasty look. Then I say, "Would you mind moving to the other side, you're sitting on my husband's side."

Housewife, 59
Her husband is an executive, 61

Every time I go into the kitchen, regardless of how many times, I have to make sure the gas is turned off.

Psychologist, male, 32

When I turn off one knob on the stove, I have to go down the row and make sure all the others are off and then do it again in the other direction.

Copywriter, male, 37

dial-a-quirk

Instead of putting names, addresses, and telephone numbers in a book, I keep clusters of small pieces of paper, corners, cards, envelope flaps, etc. in my pocket. They may not look organized, but every time I pull out the entire wad, I can go right to the one I need!

Freelance manager, male, 26

I keep telephone numbers in my head rather than on a piece of paper. The paper can get crushed or lost so I try to memorize just about every number.

House painter, male, 35

It's terribly irritating when people call my place of business after six o'clock. I've worked hard enough all day. When I answer, I say very seriously, "This is the Brooklyn Morgue. Do you have a corpse to report?" It's not quite what people expect to hear and I smirk to myself with delight at their stunned silence. It's my vicious way of retaliating.

Wholesaler, womens' apparel, male, 35

In my address book, I never write down peoples' full names, only their initials because I'm lazy. At the time I write them down I think I'll remember them so I have this book full of initials and phone numbers and I have no idea who these people are.

Stock reporter, male, 29

I have to check the telephone each night before I go to sleep to see if it's working. In case I get a call, I don't want to miss it.

Secretary, female, 29

I hang up the receiver of our wall phone upside down with the speaking part on the hanger. This way I know who used the phone last because my wife doesn't do it that way.

Court officer, male, 26

When my friend would like to end a telephone conversation, she says, "Anyhoo" and I know she's ready to say goodbye.

Housewife, 42
Her friend is a housewife, 47

In a business situation I find myself standing up when I talk on the phone. And I'm not that short! It gives me a feeling of superiority and control over the situation.

Vice president, textile business, male, 37

Whenever I'm in a strange city, I go through the telephone directory to see if there's anyone with the same last name as mine. I'm always hoping to discover a new relative. Once I called someone and she turned out to be a distant relative of my mother's.

Management analyst, female, 31

If the telephone receiver is hung up with the wires crossed, I go nuts. I try my best to be civil when a guest does it. I'll say something like, "Would you mind turning the receiver around?" and make a joke out of it. If the guilty party is someone I know well, I'll say, "What are you, crazy? Look how you hung up the phone. Fix the damn thing!"

Statistician, female, 35

I never answer a telephone between rings, only in the process of a ring because I assume people don't hang up in the middle of a ring. I don't. Whoever is calling me is more likely to be on the other end.

Media Planner, ad agency, male, 26

I hang up on answering machines. They're obnoxious.

Pharmacist, male, 34

My friend has a psychological need to be the last one to hang up the phone. I only noticed it recently although I've known him for a long time. So now I play games with him. The close of the conversation goes something like this, Me: "Goodbye." Him: "Goodbye." Me: "See you." Him: "See you." Long pause. Me: "You still there?" But it's a losing battle. He'll just wait it out.

Theatre publicist, female, 28
Her friend is a salesman, 34

SCORE:

The voyeur in you should have had a ball with this chapter because there's a whole conglomeration of goodies here. If you've checked over these other people and found yourself instead, score yourself as follows:

Twenty or less—You're probably from a little town in the Midwest.

Twenty-one to forty—A definite New Yorker.

Over forty—I wouldn't admit that if I were you. Lie. And stop twirling your hair.

and **I** thought
I was crazy!

about the author

Judy Reiser is an art director living and working in New York. Writing this book was one of her quirks. She now has many more.